The Workbook on
Christians
Under
Construction
and in
Recovery

Unless otherwise indicated scripture quotations are from The New Revised Standard Version of the Bible, copyright © 1989 by the Division of Christian Education of the National Council of the Churches of Christ in the United States of America. Used by permission.

Scripture quotations designated RSV are from the Revised Standard Version of the Bible, copyrighted 1946, 1952, and © 1971 by the Division of Christian Education, National Council of the Churches of Christ in the United States of America, and are used by permission.

Scripture quotations designated PHILLIPS are from THE NEW TESTAMENT IN MODERN ENGLISH by J. B. Phillips 1958. Used by permission of The Macmillan Company.

Scripture quotations designated NKJV are from The New King James Version. Copyright © 1979, 1980, 1982, Thomas Nelson, Inc.

The designation KJV is used throughout this book to identify quotations from the King James Version of the Bible.

The publisher gratefully acknowledges permission to reprint the following excerpts:

Excerpt from "Acquired Immunity," used by permision of Rodney E. Wilmoth.

Excerpts from "On Being Assertive," used by permission of Donald Shelby.

Excerpt from *Touchstones: A Book of Daily Meditations for Men.* ©1986 Hazelden Foundation. Used by permission.

Excerpts from "When Being Good Is Bad for You," used by permission of Bob Olmstead.

Cover design: John Robinson
Cover photograph: Byron Jorjorian
First printing: July 1993 (20)
ISBN: 0-8358-0683-9

Printed in the United States of America

THE WORKBOOK ON
Christians
Under
Construction
and in
Recovery

Maxie Dunnam

UPPER
ROOM BOOKS
NASHVILLE

To

Christians in recovery

and

the entire recovering community

at Christ United Methodist Church,

who have taught me, loved me, responded

to my ministry, and shown me the transforming

power of Jesus Christ.

CONTENTS

INTRODUCTION

THERE IS A FASCINATING STORY ABOUT A YOUNG MAN, barely twenty years old, who was caught one day stealing sheep. He was charged and convicted. As a penalty, the villagers decided to make an example out of him. They took a branding iron and branded his forehead with the letters *ST*—meaning of course, *Sheep Thief*. The brand was permanent and a constant source of shame to the young man. Penitent, he turned to God. He asked God for forgiveness. He asked God to help him overcome his problem. He was determined not to be remembered as a thief.

With courage and with God's help, he began to live in a new way, giving to others, helping others in every way. He performed endless small acts of kindness for everyone. He was thoughtful, helpful, compassionate, caring, generous, and always dependable. Years and years went by, and of course he became an old man. One day a visitor came to the village. He saw this elderly man and wondered about the letters on his forehead. He asked the people of the village what the "ST" on the man's forehead stood for. Strangely, no one could remember, but they suspected that the "ST" was an abbreviation for the word *SAINT*.

Though it may be apocryphal, it's a wonderful story. It could happen to any of us—we can act our way into a different lifestyle; indeed, we can act our way into wholeness. The ultimate possibility is that we can act our way into Christ-likeness.

The story provides a good picture of the goal of this workbook. For seven weeks we will pursue the theme: *CHRISTIANS UNDER CONSTRUCTION AND IN RECOVERY.*

Have you seen that poster that says, "Be patient with me—God is not finished with me yet"? That's what this workbook is about: the fact that we are all in process, under construction. We will also be looking at some specific recovery issues, issues with which folks who are recovering from alcohol and other drug addictions will immediately identify. Though usually associated with persons in recovery, these issues are relevant to all of us. Most of us are engaged in some process of recovery.

Gerald May, a psychiatrist and spiritual guide on the staff of The Shalem Institute for Spiritual Formation in Washington, D.C., has written a book entitled *Addiction and Grace.* In it he says that addiction is "the sacred disease of our time." Addiction is "any compulsive, habitual behavior that limits the freedom of human desire. It is caused by the attachment, or nailing, of desire to specific objects."

All human beings have an inborn desire for God. This desire may be diverted—indeed it is more often than not—to other specific things, and addiction results. We try to fulfill our desire and longing for God, which we may not recognize as such, through people, possessions, attitudes, or patterns of behavior. So, we are all in need of recovery—all under construction, if we are Christian.

May says, "When we do begin to claim our choices in response to our hunger for God, we have begun an intentional spiritual life." He calls this "homecoming." Others have called it *ongoing conversion.* That's what this workbook is about.

We will not deal with all the issues. We may not deal with the issues you think most important. However, I do believe that what we will consider here is close to the life of most of us. I'm certain of this: if you deal with these issues responsibly, you will be better equipped to grapple with other concerns and overcome other addictions and troubling problems of inner-personal and interpersonal relations.

Let's look at the process of this workbook. It is simple, but it has proven very effective.

The Plan

I have found in my many years of teaching and ministry with small groups that a six- to eight-week period for a group study is the most manageable and effective. Also, I have learned that persons can best appropriate content and truth in small doses. That is the reason for organizing the material in segments to be read daily.

The plan for this workbook is the same as for the previous ones I have written. It calls for a seven-week commitment. You are asked to give thirty minutes each day to learn about and appropriate ideals and disciplines for your transformation and growth. For most persons, the thirty minutes will come at the beginning of the day. However, if it is not possible for you to give the time at the beginning of the day, do it whenever the time is available, but do it regularly. The purpose of this spiritual journey must not be forgotten: to incorporate the content into your daily life.

Although this is an individual journey, my hope is that you will share it with some fellow pilgrims who will meet together once a week during the seven weeks of the study.

The workbook is arranged into seven major divisions, each designed to guide you for one week. These divisions contain seven sections, one for each day of the week. Each day will have three major aspects: reading about the discipline, reflecting and recording ideas and thoughts about the material and your own journey, and finally, some practical suggestions for incorporating ideas from the reading material into your daily life.

In each day's section, you will read about the common problems and needs and/or possibilities for transformation and direction for growth. It won't be too much to read but it will be enough to link you with the challenges of your recovery and growth—problems, experiences, relationships, and situations with which we must cope. Included in the reading will be portions of scripture, the basic resource for Christian discipline and living. Quotations from most sources other than scripture are followed by the author's name and page number on which each quote can be found. These citations are keyed to the *Notes* section at the back of the workbook, where you will find a complete bibliography, should you wish to read certain works more fully.

Throughout the workbook you will see this symbol ♥. When you come to the symbol, *please stop.* Do not read any further. Think and reflect as you are requested to do in order to internalize the ideas being shared or the experience reflected upon.

Reflecting and Recording

After the reading each day, there will be a time for reflecting and recording. This dimension calls you to record some of your reflections. The degree of meaning you receive from this workbook is largely dependent upon your faithfulness to its practice. You may be unable on a particular day to do precisely what is requested. If so, then simply record that fact and make a note of why you can't follow through. This may give you some insight about yourself and help you to grow.

Also, on some days there may be more suggestions than you can deal with in the time you have. Do what is most meaningful for you, and do not feel guilty.

The emphasis in this workbook is upon growth, not perfection. Don't feel guilty if you do not follow the pattern of the days exactly. Follow the content and direction seriously, but not slavishly.

Finally, always remember that this is a personal pilgrimage. What you write in your personal workbook is your private property. You may not wish to share it with anyone. For this reason, no two people should attempt to share the same workbook. The importance of what you write is not what it may mean to someone else, but what it means to you. Writing, even if it is only brief notes or single-word reminders, helps us clarify our feelings and thinking.

The significance of the reflecting and recording dimension will grow as you move along. Even beyond the seven weeks, you will find meaning in looking back to what you wrote on a particular day in response to a particular situation.

Sharing with Others

John Wesley believed that Christian "conferencing" was a means of grace for Christians. By Christian conferencing he simply meant Christians sharing intentionally their Christian experience and understanding in deliberate and serious conversation. He designed the "class meeting" as a vehicle for this discipline. In such a fellowship of Christian conversation and shared life, "one loving heart sets another on fire." The content and dynamic of this workbook will be more meaningful if you share it with others. As you share with others your own insight will be sharpened. Others will become a source of encouragement and a catalyst for change. Your weekly gathering can be that kind of means of grace. A guide for group sharing is included in the text at the end of each week.

If this is a group venture, all persons should begin their personal involvement with the workbook on the same day, so that when you come together to share as a group, you all will have been dealing with the same material and will be at the same place in the text. It will be helpful if you have an initial get-acquainted group meeting to begin the adventure. A guide for this meeting is provided in this introduction.

Group sessions for this workbook are designed to last one and one-half hours (with the exception of the initial meeting). Those sharing in the group should covenant to attend all sessions unless an emergency prevents attendance. There will be seven weekly sessions in addition to this first get-together time.

A group consisting of eight to twelve members is about the right size. Larger numbers will tend to limit individual involvement.

One person may provide the leadership for the entire seven weeks, or leaders may be assigned from week to week. The leader's task is to:

1. Read the directions and determine ahead of time how to handle the session. It may not be possible to use all the suggestions for sharing and praying together. Feel free to select those you think will be most meaningful and those for which you have adequate time.

2. Model a style of openness, honesty, and warmth. A leader should not ask others to share what he or she is not willing to share. Usually the leader should be the first to share, especially as it relates to personal experiences.

3. Moderate the discussion.

4. Encourage reluctant members to participate, and try to prevent the same few persons from doing all the talking.

5. Keep the sharing centered in personal experience, rather than academic debate.

6. Honor the time schedule. If it appears necessary to go longer than one and one-half hours, the leader should get consensus for continuing another twenty or thirty minutes.

7. See that the meeting time and place are known by all, especially if meetings are held in different homes.

8. Make sure that the necessary materials for meetings are available and that the meeting room is arranged ahead of time.

It is a good idea for weekly meetings to be held in the homes of the participants. (Hosts or hostesses should make sure there are as few interruptions as possible from children, telephone, pets, and so forth.) If the meetings are held in a church they should be in an informal setting. Participants are asked to dress casually, to be comfortable and relaxed.

If refreshments are served, they should come *after* the formal meeting. In this way, those who wish to stay longer for informal discussion may do so, while those who need to keep to the specific time schedule will be free to leave, but will get the full value of the meeting time.

Suggestions for Initial Get-Acquainted Meeting

Since the initial meeting is for the purpose of getting acquainted and beginning the shared pilgrimage, here is a good way to get started.

1. Have each person in the group give his or her full name and the name by which each wishes to be called. Do away with titles. Address all persons by their first name or nickname. If name tags are needed, provide them. Each person should make a list of the names somewhere in his or her workbook.

2. Let each person in the group share one of the happiest, most exciting, or most meaningful experiences he or she has had during the past three or four weeks. After everyone has shared in this way, let the entire group sing the Doxology or a chorus of praise.

3. After this experience of happy sharing, ask each person who will to share his or her expectation of this workbook study. Why did he or she become a part of it? What does each expect to gain from it? What are the reservations?

4. The leader should now review the introduction to the workbook and ask if there are questions about directions and procedures. (The leader should have read the introduction prior to the meeting.) If persons have not received copies of the workbook, the books should be handed out now. Remember that every person must have his or her own workbook.

5. **DAY ONE** in the workbook is the day following this initial meeting, and the next meeting should be held on **DAY SEVEN** of the first week. If a group must choose a weekly meeting other than seven days from this initial session, the reading assignment should be adjusted so that the weekly meetings are always on **DAY SEVEN**, and **DAY ONE** is always the day following a weekly meeting.

6. Nothing binds members together more than praying for one another. The leader should encourage each participant to write the

names of persons in the group in his or her workbook, and commit to praying for them by name daily the seven weeks.

7. After checking to see that everyone knows the time and place of the next meeting, the leader should close with a prayer, thanking God for each person in the group, for the opportunity for growth, and for the possibility of growing spiritual disciplines.

One final note: If someone in the group has an instant camera, ask him or her to bring it to the group meeting the next week. Be prepared to take a picture of each person in the group to be used as an aid to prayer.

WEEK ONE

Getting Ourselves Off Our Hands

PROCESS, NOT PERFECTION

Not that I have already obtained this or have already reached the goal; but I press on to make it my own, because Christ Jesus has made me his own. Beloved, I do not consider that I have made it my own; but this one thing I do: forgetting what lies behind and straining forward to what lies ahead, I press on toward the goal for the prize of the heavenly call of God in Christ Jesus. Let those of us then who are mature be of the same mind; and if you think differently about anything, this too God will reveal to you. Only let us hold fast to what we have attained.

—Philippians 3:12–16

TWO BOYS WERE PLAYING ON A BICYCLE—both riding at the same time, neither enjoying it very much. Finally, one of them said to the other, "You know, one of us could have a lot more fun if you would get off."

That's a good point, isn't it? The big idea of this week is that nothing would help us more than to *get ourselves off our own hands.*

Think about the image. We talk about getting the burden off our shoulders, or refusing to carry the problem or question in our own hands. Using those images, we are talking about refusing to take responsibility that doesn't rightly belong to us. A neurotic stance is that of always taking responsibility, always accepting the burden that doesn't belong to us. And we do that with our lives—we live as though the whole burden of living is in our hands. We need to *get ourselves off our own hands.*

That's where the scripture quoted above would take us. Paul knew that *process*, not *perfection*, was the name of the game of life. Isn't that what he is saying in verse 12?

> Not that I have already obtained this or have already reached the goal; but I press on to make it my own, because Christ Jesus has made me his own.

The King James Version and the original Revised Standard Version use the word *perfect*: "Not that I am already perfect."

Perfectionism is one of the great barriers to wholeness. For many of us, this is a great burden. In the process of growing up, we have gotten the notion that we must *be perfect* if we are to be loved and accepted by others, if we are going to be who God created us to be. One of the biggest problems is that we don't know what perfection looks like, yet we have to choose models. We do so, and end up trying to be like someone else. Often we nullify our own uniqueness and stifle our discovery of wholeness, because we are imitating the limitations of others.

Perfectionism will be an ongoing concern in this workbook journey. For now, it is enough for us to accept the witness of Paul: "I press on!" Perfection is not what life is about; in fact, some would say perfection is nonexistent among humans.

Life is process, change, growth, movement. If perfection is possible, it is gift and grace, not something we attain.

Reflecting and Recording

♥ When you come to a sign like this *stop* and spend time in reflection before reading further.

Look back over your life. What messages about perfection were you taught by your parents? Make some notes here.

What lessons about perfection were you taught by other important persons in your life? Make some notes on the next page.

Perfectionism can be *caught* as well as taught. Think about how, though you were not explicitly taught to be perfect, you caught this message from someone you loved and wanted to please.

During the Day

Move through the day seeking to be sensitive to how your *perfectionism* influences your actions, attitudes, and especially your relationships.

Day Two

"CHRIST JESUS HAS MADE ME HIS OWN"

IT IS NOT EXTERNAL THINGS THAT COUNT, but what has happened and is happening inside. Yesterday, we gave attention to Paul's witness which suggests that process, not perfection, is the name of the game of life.

Not that I have already obtained this or have already reached the goal; but I press on to make it my own, because Christ Jesus has made me his own.

—Philippians 3:12

Consider the context in which Paul makes his confession.

> For it is we who are the circumcision, who worship in the Spirit of God and boast in Christ Jesus and have no confidence in the flesh—even though I, too, have reason for confidence in the flesh.
>
> If anyone else has reason to be confident in the flesh, I have more: circumcised on the eighth day, a member of the people of Israel, of the tribe of Benjamin, a Hebrew born of Hebrews; as to the law, a Pharisee; as to zeal, a persecutor of the church; as to righteousness under the law, blameless.
>
> Yet whatever gains I had, these I have come to regard as loss because of Christ. More than that, I regard everything as loss because of the surpassing value of knowing Christ Jesus my Lord. For his sake I have suffered the loss of all things, and I regard them as rubbish, in order that I may gain Christ and be found in him, not having a righteousness of my own that comes from the law, but one that comes through faith in Christ, the righteousness from God based on faith. I want to know Christ and the power of his resurrection and the sharing of his sufferings by becoming like him in his death, if somehow I may attain the resurrection from the dead.
>
> Not that I have already obtained this or have already reached the goal; but I press on to make it my own, because Christ Jesus has made me his own.
>
> —Philippians 3:3-12

There is a lesson here about perfection, about basing our sense of worthiness on *performance*. Paul is sharing this new perspective that has radically changed his life: "Whatever gains I had, these I have come to regard as loss because of Christ" (verse 7).

Note the plural *gains*, and the singular *loss*. This is a revealing contrast. The outward privileges Paul catalogues had at one time been distinct and separate gains, performances that gave him meaning. Now they were one big bundle of loss—loss because in his mind they were useless now; or, as Phillips translates it, "useless rubbish."

"Righteousness . . . from the law" as Paul calls it (performance, perfection, *doing* good in order to *be* good, keeping the rules) is illusory, short-lived: now you have it, now you don't. We can never gain salvation (wholeness) in that way.

But there is a way to growth, wholeness, transformation, and ultimate salvation: "knowing Christ Jesus my Lord". . . and being "found in Him" (verses 8, 9). Paul can press on, grow, and change "because Christ Jesus has made me his own" (verse 12).

Because Christ Jesus has made us his own, we can *get ourselves off our own hands.* We don't do our good deeds *in order to be accepted* by Christ; we do them because we *have been accepted* by Christ. Our faith in Jesus Christ as Savior and our commitment to Him as Lord puts us in relationship with Christ.

If we named modern musicians who we thought had achieved perfection, Artur Rubinstein would be among them. In his eighties, he had reached greater heights than he had known in his long career as an almost peerless artist. After long years of impeccable performance, he still kept his interpretations fresh and inspiring. Rubinstein claimed a "secret power" took over when he played, which made every occasion a new moment for him.

I would have liked to question Rubinstein about that "secret power." Persons who know Christ, whom "Christ Jesus has made . . . his own" have a wonderful source of power and wholeness.

Reflecting and Recording

Spend some time reflecting on the changes that would happen in your life if you moved to a deeper understanding and commitment to the fact that Christ Jesus has made you his own.

♥ (Remember when you come to a sign like this you are to spend time in reflection before moving on in your reading.)

Write a few sentences to remind you later of what your reflections today were.

During the Day

When you feel called upon today *to prove yourself,* flavor your reaction and response by claiming the fact that Christ Jesus has made you his own.

Day Three

LIVE ONE DAY AT A TIME: PROCRASTINATION

But if God so clothes the grass of the field, which is alive today and tomorrow is thrown into the oven, will he not much more clothe you—you of little faith? Therefore do not worry, saying, 'What will we eat?' or 'What will we drink?' or 'What will we wear?' For it is the Gentiles who strive for all these things; and indeed your heavenly Father knows that you need all these things. But strive first for the kingdom of God and his righteousness, and all these things will be given to you as well. So do not worry about tomorrow, for tomorrow will bring worries of its own. Today's trouble is enough for today.

—Matthew 6:30–34

MY FRIEND, BILL HINSON TELLS OF A WOMAN who shared with her housekeeper some of the things that were tearing her life apart.

She confessed to her housekeeper, "I feel like I'm falling apart. I'm not a woman. I'm a mob. There are so many of me that I'm going off in all different directions. I'm overextended. I have far too many commitments, too many things out there waiting for me to do."

Finally, at the end of her tirade, she said, "I guess I just have too many irons in the fire."

Her housekeeper, who had been ironing all the while and listening to that outpouring of confusion, without so much as looking up, said to her, "Well, then, iron with the one that's hottest!" (Hinson, p. 21).

Quaint, but life-changing wisdom: "Iron with the one that's hottest." Jesus would say "amen" to this guidance. That's what he was teaching us in the Sermon on the Mount.

This doesn't mean we become completely task-oriented. We will examine later the problems brought by that narrow orientation to life. Yet, if we are going to get ourselves off our hands, we must concentrate on the issues at hand, the issues with which we can deal today.

Two things happen that make life an intolerable burden to us. One, we procrastinate. We put off doing something that needs to be done today, or we refuse to deal with a problem that is plaguing us now. Procrastination is the thief of time. Things that need to be done pile up and become a big load we can't possibly carry. So we end up mentally flogging ourselves, seeing ourselves as incapable, unable to perform. The fallout of procrastination is anxiety and stress. Our stress level rises and we become anxious about what is going to happen because we haven't done what was needed.

Consider the possibility that it may be your perfectionism that is paralyzing you. If you can't do the job perfectly, why do it at all? If you think you can't handle the relationship—that you won't be comfortable in it—why take the risk? Maybe you are angry at the expectations of others.

Whatever the cause, procrastination is crippling. As long as we procrastinate, we keep our life in our hands.

Reflecting and Recording

I've come to believe that lying to ourselves may be more deeply ingrained than lying to others. Reflect on to what degree you believe that to be true.

♥

Why do you procrastinate? Be honest. How does it relate to your perfectionism?

♥

List two things you need to do today that you may be tempted to put off:

1.

2.

Make a plan for doing them.

Spend some time in prayer for the persons who may be involved in what you need to do, and for strength and guidance for yourself.

During the Day

At 10 A.M., noon, and 3 P.M., check yourself on what you have done about the two priorities for today.

| Day Four |

LIVE ONE DAY AT A TIME: ANTICIPATION

YESTERDAY, WE NOTED THAT TWO THINGS make life an intolerable burden for us because they prevent us from living one day at a time. We considered the first: procrastination.

The second is *anticipation*.

Go back and read Matthew 6:30–34, which was printed for Day Three.

Jesus knew that anticipation was debilitating. "Do not worry about tomorrow, for tomorrow will bring worries of its own." That ought to shock us out of our thinking that tomorrow is going to be better. The truth is that it is probably going to be very much like today, and if we aren't excited about today, we won't be excited tomorrow.

Anticipation expresses itself in two problematic ways. The first we have just noted: Tomorrow may look so inviting, alluring, and challenging that we will be seduced away from living life today. Or, we may think of tomorrow as an escape. Since we have a tomorrow, we'll muddle through today and get on to the business of living then.

An opposite problem may also be brought on by anticipation. Rather than seeing tomorrow as an escape, or an inviting challenge, we may morbidly see it as something to dread. This is the more common problem: anticipating, and thus worrying, about things that never happen.

I recently had a physical examination. Some of the tests had to be analyzed later. Three days later, my doctor called to say he had found something that aroused his concern, so he wanted to do two other tests. He told me he was "being conservative" and that I should not be concerned.

My pace and schedule is horrendous. It took two weeks, leaving my calendar as it was, to set up a time for the additional tests. Two days later, in my prayer time, I thought, "How foolish! What if something *is* wrong?" Then it hit me. "You are working on a workbook on growth and recovery, and one issue is 'borrowing trouble,' anticipating the worst. Practice what you preach."

The Lord was gracious. I did not think of those tests again until my prayer time the preceding morning before tests. They turned out fine— but what if they hadn't? Anticipating the worst would have made it worse. There is nothing redemptive about borrowing tomorrow's problems. Neither is there anything generous about future promises as a substitute for living and giving yourself today.

Reflecting and Recording

List three or four things you are concerned about that cause you to worry.

Are you keeping your life on your hands by spending too much energy anticipating the worst that could happen?

Is there some relationship, some involvement you are ignoring because you anticipate tomorrow being better?

♥

During the Day

Remember the possibility I suggested yesterday—that lying to ourselves may be more deeply ingrained in us than lying to others. Test the probability of that as you move through the day, tempted to procrastinate and/or anticipate.

Day Five

BREAKING THE BACK OF OUR OWN EGO

IF WE ARE GOING TO GET OURSELVES OFF OUR HANDS, we must break the back of our own ego. Though we are responsible for the decisions we make, life is ultimately in God's hands. Paul gives us a good perspective in his Letter to the Romans.

> I appeal to you therefore, brothers and sisters, by the mercies of God, to present your bodies as a living sacrifice, holy and acceptable to God, which is your spiritual worship. Do not be conformed to this world, but be transformed by the renewing of your minds, so that you may discern what is the will of God—what is good and acceptable and perfect. For by the grace given to me I say to everyone among you not to think of yourself more highly than you ought to think, but to think with sober judgment, each according to the measure of faith that God has assigned. For as in one body we have many members, and not all the members have the same function, so we, who are many, are one body in Christ, and individually we are members one of another. We have gifts that differ according to the grace given to us: prophecy, in proportion to faith; ministry, in ministering; the teacher, in teaching; the exhorter,

in exhortation; the giver, in generosity; the leader, in diligence; the compassionate, in cheerfulness.

—Romans 12:1-8

The reason we think we have the total responsibility and bear the total burden of our living is our ego. We think more highly of ourselves than we ought to think. What a burden our ego is!

How much emotional energy do you spend protecting yourself from every possible slight, challenging every word spoken by either friend or enemy which demeans you, cringing under every cool look, tossing at night because someone else seemed preferred over you? How much emotional energy do you spend trying to doctor up your image and "look good," trying to say only what's "cool," trying to do only what's accepted, trying to appear only in a way that will make you admired, trying to sustain a subtle publicity campaign that says you are more, do more, have more . . . ?

Exhausting, isn't it?

It's a cruel, crushing burden, and it never lets up. It never lets you relax a minute to recoup. It wears away your strength, your morale, your life. We may call it "stress," but its real name is "ego."

Ego may be open or subtle, worldly or Christianized. It may mean smashing enough faces and brains to wow the world of boxing. It may mean taking over enough companies to wow the corporate world of business. It may mean getting enough church members or adherents to wow the religious world. Or individually, memorizing the most verses, visiting the most shut-ins, teaching the biggest Bible class—whatever makes the rest say "wow!"

Or ego may mean writhing and seething because you *haven't* made it to the top: you lost the match, your company was outclassed, your ministry is struggling. . . .

Ego keeps you forever tense and dissatisfied, forever in agony lest someone else appear better, smarter, richer, more liked, more successful, more admired, more spiritual, more "blessed." . . .

Ego is a terrible, terrible burden. (Ortlund, pp. 64-65)

Well, how do we deal with it? We have to break the back of our own ego. But how do we do that? Anne Ortlund suggests a direction by pointing to what at first seemed a strange word of scripture in relation to the issue of ego—the promise of Jesus:

Come to me, all who labor and are heavy laden, and I will give you rest. Take my yoke upon you, and learn from me; for I am gentle and lowly in heart, and you will find rest for your souls. For my yoke is easy, and my burden is light.

—Matthew 11:28–30, RSV

Ortlund suggests that the burden Jesus wants to remove is the burden we manufacture ourselves, with our own ego. Most of us who carry that burden are heavy laden; we are dragged down and depressed and discouraged and exhausted by it all our lives.

Jesus says, "Let me give you rest. Learn of Me. I am meek!"

Meekness is the opposite of ego with its pretense, pride, competition.

"I will give you rest," He says. "Accept the blessed relief of being only what you are. Then I can do it all!"

"Quit pretending. Quit striving. My dear child, quit trying to be some cocky little god competing with Me—maybe, worst of all, some cocky little *religious* god. Come down off your silly, rickety throne."

"Only my Father is worthy of a throne! Bow to Him only, and give Him all the glory, and let Him be all and do all in you and for you!" (Ortlund, p. 65)

That's in harmony with what Paul was saying, do not "think of yourself more highly than you ought to think." And remember his own confession, "Christ Jesus has made me his own." We don't have to bear all the burden of living by ourselves. To think we do is egotistical arrogance. And to get ourselves off our hands, we need to break the back of our own ego.

Reflecting and Recording

Our ego expresses itself in a lot of ways. The following is far from an exhaustive list of the different selves we are. Check two that you readily identify as an expression of yourself.

_____ Male Macho Self   _____ Always-right self

_____ Female Macho Self   _____ Afraid-to-risk self

_____ Must-be-in-control self   _____ What-I-possess-is-who-
                                          I-am self

Spend some time reflecting on these two expressions of yourself that tell you about the need to break the back of your own ego.

During the Day

Before you leave this time of reflection, review the list of different expressions of self. As you move through the day, be attentive, not just to the two you checked, but other self-expressions that may be your ego keeping yourself on your hands. Try to break the pattern.

Day Six

GUARDING OUR LIVES

BILL HINSON, WHOM I QUOTED EARLIER, tells of an expression they used in elementary school when he was growing up.

When someone began to bully another, the courageous thing to say (in spite of the fact that you might be scared to death) was, "I'm like a turnip patch. You can have a mess of me any time you want it!" That's the way Jesus was. He was like a turnip patch. You could have a mess of him any time you wanted him. He was available.

This was his understanding of life.

> Then he said to them all, "If any want to become my followers, let them deny themselves and take up their cross daily and follow me. For those who want to save their life will lose it, and those who lose their life for my sake will save it. What does it profit them if they gain the whole world, but lose or forfeit themselves?"
>
> —Luke 9:23-25

The reason we keep life in our own hands is that we are guarding it. We want to protect it. We don't want people to demand too much. We don't want to be vulnerable and risk.

Too many of us have an "imposition complex" (Hinson). We are afraid that people are going to impose on us. So we guard our life. We don't pray daily that God will use us—and show us ways to pour out our life for God's glory and the good of others. We guard our lives, and so we keep ourselves on our own hands.

Many people are familiar with the columns of Erma Bombeck. When she was interviewed on a television talk show several years ago, the host asked her if she saved any ideas so that she would be assured of at least one strong column each week. Her reply is vintage Bombeck . . . and instructive:

> I don't save anything. My pockets are empty at the end of a week. So is my refrigerator. So is my gas tank. So is my file of "ideas." I trot out the best I've got, and come the next week, I bargain, whimper, make promises, cower, and throw myself on the mercy of the Almighty for just "three more columns" in exchange for cleaning my oven.
>
> I didn't get to this point overnight. I came from a family of savers who were sired by poverty, raised in the Depression, and worshipped at the altar of self-denial. Throughout the

years, I've seen a fair number of my family who have died leaving candles that have never been lit, appliances that never got out of the box, and new sofas shrouded in chenille bedspreads.

I always had a dream that when I am asked to give an accounting of my life to a higher court, it will go thusly: "So, empty your pockets. What have you got left of your life? Any dreams that were unfulfilled? Any unused talent that we gave you when you were born that you still have left? Any unpaid compliments or bits of love that you haven't spread around?" And I will answer, "I've nothing to return, I spent everything you gave me. . . ." (Bauknight, February 26, 1989)

I believe Bombeck is on course. We can't hoard life or store up all our resources for tomorrow. To get ourselves off our own hands we need to quit guarding life.

Reflecting and Recording

Spend some time thinking about how you may be guarding your life.

Focus on the way you spend your time. Is there any indication from your time use that you are guarding your life?

Think of some experience of the past three weeks when you refused some "call" on your life. Write enough about that experience to get it clearly in your mind.

If you feel a need, pray that God will forgive you for "guarding your life."

Are you sharing this workbook journey with others? If so, do you have a list of their names? Are you praying daily for them?

During the Day
Be on guard today against guarding your life.

Day Seven

CIRCLES OF ACCEPTANCE

THE CARTOONIST JULES FEIFFER CAPTURES, in his backhanded style, the meaning of relationship in his work. In a series of cartoon drawings, he pictures husband and wife, sitting blandly face to face in their living room. The woman is listlessly turning the pages of a magazine. The man is playing with an empty martini glass. There is no conversation or contact. The man breaks the stagnant silence by asking a profound question.

"Do you believe in life after death?"

The woman doesn't move. Her emotionless expression remains the same and she continues to gaze blankly at her magazine. But she does answer, and her answer is more profound than the question.

"What do you call this?"

No communication, no conversation, no contact between living, breathing persons is "life after death." To get ourselves off our own hands we need circles of acceptance, other persons with whom we can trust our feelings and fears, our hopes and dreams, our failures and victories. Karen Horney, the psychologist, says we may run toward others, run away from them, or hole up somewhere in the middle. None of those responses contribute to wholeness. The essence of identity is in relationship with others.

Two things happen when we participate in circles of acceptance that move us out of our self and get us off our hands. One, we surrender some of our freedom. (This helps also in breaking the back of our own ego.) When we make a commitment to others we are no longer unattached; we are living *with* others.

In commitment to others, I am no longer a separate *I*. Others are a part of the definition of who I am.

Two, we surrender control. By our choice we allow others to have a claim on our lives. As we considered yesterday, we cease guarding our lives.

Control is also an ego issue. Surrendering control is a way of dealing with the problem of ego.

Reflecting and Recording

Name three or four people whom you would consider your circle of acceptance.

1.   3.
2.   4.

Concentrate on each one of them for a couple of minutes. How do they make your life better?

If you are not a part of a group sharing this workbook journey, you may want to invite a few people to join you. You could be the initial leader. Call them together and share this venture with them. (Read the introduction about such groups.)

If you are a part of a group, this will become a circle of acceptance. These people will be sharing their life with you, and you with them. Pray for them now.

During the Day

Call at least one (all if possible) of the people you named above as your circle of acceptance. Thank them for what they mean to you.

GROUP MEETING FOR WEEK ONE

Introduction

These group sessions will be most meaningful as they reflect the experience of all the participants. This guide is simply an effort to facilitate personal sharing. Therefore, do not be rigid in following these suggestions. The leader, especially, should seek to be sensitive to what is going on in the lives of the participants and to focus the group sharing on those experiences. Ideas are important. We should wrestle with new ideas as well as with ideas with which we disagree. It is important, however, that the group meeting not become a debate about ideas. The emphasis should be on persons—experiences, feelings, and meaning.

As the group comes to the place where all can share honestly and openly what is happening in their lives, the experience will become more meaningful. This does not mean sharing only the good or positive; share also struggles, the difficulties, the negatives.

Discipline is not easy; it is deceptive to pretend that it is. Growth requires effort. Don't be afraid to share your questions, reservations, and "dry periods," as well as those things in which you find meaning.

Our themes of construction and recovery indicate that we are all growing, have varying needs, and are at different places on our Christian journey. That should be acknowledged, affirmed, and celebrated. The sooner and more freely each person shares personally, the more helpful you will be to each other. Remember, you are a unique gift to the group. You have something to give that no one else can offer.

Sharing Together

1. You may begin your time together by allowing time for each person in the group to share his or her most meaningful day with the workbook this week. The leader should begin this sharing. Tell why that particular day was so meaningful.

2. Now share your most difficult day. Tell what you experienced and why it was so difficult.

3. As a group, spend five to ten minutes talking about to what degree you are a perfectionist and how you were taught it.

4. Spend five to ten minutes sharing responses to the statement on Day Three, that "lying to ourselves may be more deeply ingrained than lying to others."

5. Invite two or three persons to share how they have spent too much time anticipating the worst that could happen . . . and it never did. (Refer to Day Four.)

6. Spend ten to fifteen minutes discussing what it would mean in your personal life if you "broke the back of our own ego." Be honest and share the ego expression of yourself which you identified on Day Five.

7. Invite two or three people to share their most recent experience of "guarding our lives."

Praying Together

Today (Day Seven) the theme was circles of acceptance. It was suggested that the group with which you are sharing this workbook study will become a circle of acceptance. This is one of the most valuable dimensions of such a venture.

At the heart of your sharing is prayer.

Each week the group is asked to pray together. Corporate prayer is one of the great blessings of Christian community. There is power in corporate prayer, and it is important that this dimension be included in our shared pilgrimage.

There is power in a community on a common journey verbalizing their thoughts and feelings to God in the presence of their fellow pilgrims. Verbal prayers should be offered spontaneously as a person chooses to pray aloud—not "let's go around the circle now, and each one pray."

It is important that you feel comfortable in this and that no pressure be placed on anyone to pray aloud. Silent corporate prayer may be as vital and meaningful as verbal corporate prayer. God does not need to hear our verbal words to hear our prayers. Silence, where thinking is centered and attention is focused, may provide our deepest periods of prayer.

Suggestions for this "Praying Together" time will be given each week. The leader for the week should regard these only as suggestions. What is happening in the meeting—the mood, the needs that are expressed, the timing—should determine the direction of the group's praying together. Here are some possibilities for this closing period.

• Let the group think back over the sharing that has taken place during this session. What personal needs or concerns came out of the sharing? Begin to speak these aloud—any person verbalizing a need or a concern that has been expressed. Don't hesitate to mention a concern that you may have picked up from another, i.e., "Mary isn't able to be with us this week because her son is in the hospital. Let's pray for her son and for her."

It will be helpful for each person to make notes of the concerns and needs that are mentioned. Enter deliberately into a period of silence. Let the leader verbalize each of these needs successively, allowing for a brief period following each so that persons in the group may center their attention and focus their prayers on the person, need, or concern mentioned. All of this will be in silence as each person prays in his or her own way.

• Let the leader close this time of sharing and silent prayer by asking the group to share in prayer liturgy. The leader will call the name of each person in the group, after which the group will say, "Lord, bless him/her" as they focus their eyes on that person. Let the person whose name is called look at each person in the room to catch their eye and receive their "look" of blessing as well as their word. When this is done, the leader calls the next name, until all are "blessed" and looked at with a blessing. Then the leader may simply say, "Amen."

Picture Taking: If someone has an instant camera (Polaroid), take a picture of each person in the group. Turn pictures face down on a table, and let each person take one. This is the person for whom you will pray specifically this week. Before you go, take a few minutes to visit with the person whose picture you chose, getting to know him or her better. Ask if there are things coming up in that person's life about which you might pray.

Bring the picture to the group meeting next week. Each week you will choose a new person for whom to pray.

Week Two

When Being Good Is Bad for You

Day One

THE HEART OF THE CHRISTIAN LIFE

"HAVE YOU BEEN WRITING ANY PERSONAL EXPERIENCE articles lately?" the woman asked the writer. "No," replied the writer, "I've been busy having them" (Ruth Peterman, quoted by Beattie, p. xi).

Most of us have been having the personal experience we will consider this week. We may not talk about it a lot, and we certainly may not write about it, but it's a common experience: the experience of codependency.

Some may not be familiar with the term. It's common in the community of those dealing with and recovering from addiction. Let's begin with a limited but suggestive definition. Codependents are people who have to *take care* of others, but the *taking-care-of* has a sick quality to it.

Many Christians are codependent in a sick way because they have a misunderstanding of what is one of the primary calls of Christian discipleship: to love and care for other people. In fact, selfless and self-sacrificing love is at the heart of the Christian life.

When I ask audiences around the nation to name the one person who best demonstrates the meaning of the Christian life, by far the most frequently mentioned person is Mother Teresa. Malcolm Muggeridge, the British lay theologian who was converted late in life, writes about her:

> In the dismal slums of Calcutta . . . Mother Teresa and her Missionaries of Charity go about Jesus's work of love with incomparable dedication. When I think of them, as I have seen them at their work and at their devotions, I want to put away all the books, tear up all the scribbled notes. There are no more doubts or dilemmas; everything is perfectly clear. What com-

40

mentary or exposition, however eloquent, lucid, perceptive, inspired even, can equal in elucidation and illumination the effect of these dedicated lives? What mind has conceived a discourse, or tongue spoken it, which conveys even to a minute degree the light they shine before men? *I was an hungered, and ye gave me meat; I was thirsty, and ye gave me drink; I was a stranger, and ye took me in; naked and ye clothed me: I was sick, and ye visited me; I was in prison, and ye came unto me*—the words come alive, as no study or meditation could possibly make them, in the fulfillment in the most literal sense of Jesus's behest to see in the suffering face of humanity his suffering face, and in their broken bodies, his.

In the face of a Mother Teresa I trace the very geography of Jesus's Kingdom; all the contours and valleys and waterways. I need no other map. (Muggeridge, pp. 73, 71)

Selfish, self-sacrificing love is at the heart of the Christian faith, and Mother Teresa is an incarnation of it. This is the way Jesus spoke about it:

As the Father has loved me, so I have loved you; abide in my love. If you keep my commandments, you will abide in my love, just as I have kept my Father's commandments and abide in his love. I have said these things to you so that my joy may be in you, and that your joy may be complete.

This is my commandment that you love one another as I have loved you. No one has greater love than this, to lay down one's life for one's friends. You are my friends if you do what I command you."

—John 15:9–14

Reflecting and Recording

Codependents are people who have to *take care* of people, but the *taking-care-of* has a sick quality to it.

This is a beginning definition of codependence. The emphasis is on *have*: people who *have* to take care of people. It's a compulsion. Caring for others gives them identity and meaning. This is the way they feel important and needed. Their need to be needed is out of proportion to the point that if they are not doing something for someone, they feel worthless.

In light of this beginning understanding, spend some time reflecting on how the Christian faith as selfless, self-sacrificing love may set us up for being codependent.

During the Day

Pay attention to your response to others and your actions. How much of what you do and how you relate is connected with your need to be needed?

> *Day Two*

GETTING INTO THE PICTURE

THE TERMS, *CODEPENDENCY* AND *CODEPENDENT* have not been around long. Bob Olmstead, a United Methodist minister in Nevada, collected the following things that have been said about codependency.

Codependents need to help other people because they have abandoned developing intrinsic meaning of their own. All their meaning comes from the outside. Without somebody to help they feel like "nothing."

Codependents are relationship addicts who frequently use a relationship in the same way drunks use alcohol: to get a "fix."

Codependents will do almost anything to stay in a relationship, regardless of how awful that relationship is, because they have little concept of a self apart from what others see in them and "need" from them. . . .

Codependents are the "good Christian martyrs." They suffer and they let you know they suffer. They maintain chaotic situations . . . by taking care of their drinkers, by making excuses, by holding their households together, cleaning up the messes, enduring the outbursts, and so on . . . when blowing the whistle would have been the truly caring thing to do!

Codependents believe that if someone in the family is unhappy or angry, they (the codependent) must have caused it and they can make it better. They do not respect others enough to allow them to work out their own problems. They promote dependence.

Codependents are so focused on other people's feelings that they lose touch with their own feelings and cannot determine what they themselves want. They just want to make everybody happy (Olmstead, June 24, 1990).

One critic of the codependency movement has said that as currently defined, it fits about 99.9 percent of the population. There is some truth in that, but that doesn't mean it is not a problem.

Reflecting and Recording

Reread the things that have been said about codependents and codependency. As you do, put a check (√) beside the ones that describe you in part or in whole. Underline words or phrases to which you might say, "Yeah, that's me," or "I've felt or done that," or "That's my temptation," or, "I'm fighting that."

If you did not check at least one of the categories or identify with some of the descriptive words or phrases, you are one outstandingly healthy person. Or, you are not being honest! Do you want to give it another try?

Read John 15:9-14 printed in yesterday's session.

Spend a few minutes in prayer in response to Christ's call, and in the awareness of what you may have learned about your tendency toward codependency.

During the Day

As suggested yesterday, move through today paying attention to how much of what you do and how you relate to others is connected to your need to be needed.

Day Three

SELFLESS, SELF-SACRIFICING LOVE CAN BE A HINDRANCE

Beloved, let us love one another, because love is from God; everyone who loves is born of God and knows God. Whoever does not love does not know God, for God is love. God's love was revealed among us in this way: God sent his only Son into the world so that we might live through him. In this is love, not that we loved God but that he loved us and sent his Son to be the atoning sacrifice for our sins. Beloved, since God loved us so much, we also ought to love one another. No one has ever seen God; if we love one another, God lives in us, and his love is perfected in us.

—1 John 4:7-12

THERE IS NO QUESTION ABOUT IT; the witness of scripture is clear: selfless, self-sacrificing love is the ultimate expression of Christian living. Sadhu Sundar Singh was an Indian Christian who is in the company of such modern witnesses to the Christian way as Mother Teresa. He was once asked, "What is life's most difficult burden?" He answered, "To have no burden to carry."

Sundar Singh is right, for this is the bottom line of Christian living: being willing to bear the burdens of others. Nothing is more beautiful and inspiring than persons who give themselves unselfishly in extravagant love to others.

Is it shocking, then, for me to say that selfless, self-sacrificing love can be a hindrance to our personal wholeness and to the health of a relationship?

Let's stay with the notion of codependency. Melody Beattie has written three classic books on this subject: *Codependent No More, Beyond Codependency and Getting Better All The Time,* and *Codependents' Guide to the Twelve Steps.* She defines codependency as being affected by someone else's behavior and obsessed with controlling it.

Do you see the possibility? Consider how we become obsessed with other people's behavior.

Focus on the area of addiction, since this is the experience in which the pervasive, destructive behavior of codependency has been so clearly identified. The astounding fact is that in the life of almost every alcoholic, workaholic, drug addict, compulsive gambler, or overspender there is also a codependent. The codependent can be a spouse, a child, a parent, or a friend obsessed with the other person's behavior. Our obsession forces us to live our lives as a reaction to the life of another.

For instance, in an alcoholic home, lying is a part of the everyday dynamic. Not only does the alcoholic lie, other members of the family (codependents) help the addict maintain his or her lie.

"We mustn't let people know about Daddy's drinking."

"Mommy's not feeling good today—let's be quiet and let her rest."

"Don't tell Grandma and Grandpa about Daddy's problem last week."

So we help the addict maintain his or her lie. One of the biggest lies is, "I can quit anytime I choose."

When our love contributes to "the lie," then our love is a hindrance to our wholeness and the wholeness of the other.

Consider the possibility of our love being controlling. That's a part of Beattie's definition of codependency: being affected by someone else's behavior and *obsessed with controlling"* (italics mine).

When we look at our love being controlling in the extreme, we may find that while our use of love for control may not be blatant, it is a negative factor in our relationships and in our growth.

In almost every dysfunctional home, control is the name of the game. Maybe a domineering, critical, legalistic, perfectionistic parent creates an oppressive cloud of control. Or perhaps a parent caught in the chains of substance abuse causes chaos. No one knows what to expect next, so there is frantic energy spent in seeking to control.

If you are an adult that has come from a family where control was a major issue, there is a good chance that you came into adulthood possessing a need to control. This is a vicious cycle.

Mixed up in all of this mess of controlling is our love. We want to control because we love. We think that we can protect our children, our spouses, our best friends, from hardship, pain, and suffering if only we can control them. When love is expressed as control, it is a hindrance to growth and relationship.

Reflecting and Recording

I've never known a relationship, even the healthiest, where the tendency to control was not present. The *need* to control is the issue. The degree to which we feel we *must* be in control is a good gauge of our wholeness.

The willingness to surrender power and control is a sign of health, not of weakness or a character flaw.

Reflect on how control might operate in a family.

The husband/father is usually physically stronger. He could use his superior strength to force the submission of his wife and children. He could—does he or did he in your family situation?

The wife/mother could withhold her love and affirmation from her children; that, and her sexual gifts, from her husband in order to control and/or coerce. She could—does she or did she in your family situation?

Children learn the game too. An extreme example is an anorexic teen who may be living under the absolute control of parents. He or she may be reversing the control factor. "I can't do what I want; you can control my activity, but I can stop eating." And who can make that teenager eat?

Children can adopt behavior that puts them in control. How is that happening, or did it happen, in your family situation?

During the Day

Seek to be aware of the occasions today when you are tempted to control. Examine whether the need to control in the situation reflects something negative about where you are in your growth as a Christian.

Day Four

Being Good Is Bad for You When You Compulsively Care for Others, but Ignore Caring for Yourself

When the Pharisees heard that he had silenced the Sadducees, they gathered together, and one of them, a lawyer, asked him a question to test him. "Teacher, which commandment in the law is the greatest?" He said to him, "'You shall love the Lord your God with all your heart, and with all your soul, and with all your mind.' This is the greatest and first commandment. And a second is like it: 'You shall love your neighbor as yourself.' On these two commandments hang all the law and the prophets."

—Matthew 22:34–40

MY MOTHER IS A COMPULSIVE CARETAKER OF OTHERS. She has spent her life taking care of her husband and her five children. All the meaning in her life has come primarily from keeping house, cooking, washing clothes, planting and cultivating a garden, canning food, always having food on the table, washing and ironing—caring for others.

She has taken caretaking to the "martyr complex" stage: doing for others when what she did was unhealthy for herself—and many times unhealthy for those for whom she was doing it. She was never aware, however, that what she was doing for others was unhealthy for them.

One of my most painful experiences is to spend time with my 87-year-old mother who can no longer care for anyone—in fact, she can hardly care for herself. Do you know what hurts her most? She can't stoop over and lift the iron skillet out of the lower kitchen cabinet and mix cornbread and cook it for her children when we go home. She can't make pallets on the floor for her grandchildren. She can't do any of those things that have given her meaning. My mother is a classic personification of a person who, without somebody to help, feels like nothing.

Do you know anybody like that? Think about it—persons who feel like nothing because they have nobody to help.

Only recently, it has come clear to me why my mother is so angry about the fact that we allowed doctors to keep her alive last year. She had heart failure and would have died twice without CPR. She's living with the help of a pacemaker, and she won't even name it. She has never called it a pacemaker. She calls it "that thing." That's how angry she is.

She's angry because in her mind she's not living. She feels like nothing because she is not able to help anyone.

Now that's extreme. But play it out in your life. Being good is bad for you when you compulsively care for others, but ignore caring for yourself.

The second great commandment, which Jesus said was like the first, is to love our neighbors as ourselves. We become sick in our serving when we try to love others, but don't love and care for ourselves.

Reflecting and Recording

Do you know anyone who feels like nothing because he or she has nobody to help? Name that person and write a paragraph describing him or her.

Consider yourself. How does what you do for others give you meaning?

To what degree are you caring for others and ignoring yourself?

During the Day

Continue to monitor your motivation for doing for others. Are you seeking to control? Are you ignoring yourself in caring for others?

Day Five

BEING GOOD IS BAD FOR YOU WHEN IT FORCES YOU TO ENDURE LIFE RATHER THAN TO LIVE IT.

So again Jesus said to them, "Very truly, I tell you, I am the gate for the sheep. All who came before me are thieves and bandits; but the sheep did not listen to them. I am the gate. Whoever enters by me will be saved, and will come in and go out and find pasture. The thief comes only to steal and kill and destroy. I came that they may have life, and have it abundantly."

—John 10:7-10

IN ITS BROADEST SCOPE, CODEPENDENCY may be defined as *an addiction to people, behaviors,* or *things.* Because of our addictions, we are driven. While we seek to control, we are really controlled by our addiction. There is a real sense in which we are trapped.

On the dust jacket of their book, *Love Is a Choice,* Robert Hemfelt, Frank Minirth, and Paul Meier record these telling statements:

"I just keep telling myself that if I try harder, I'll be able to fix him."

"It feels as if we have been battling for control since the day we met, and I have no idea who is winning or losing."

"I spend all of my time and energy doing all the right things and trying to please everyone. And yet, at the end of the day, I still feel guilty. Why?"

"I vowed I'd never marry a man like Dad. But here I am married to a man who is married to his job, just like Dad."

Then there is this revealing word: "If you identify with any of these statements, you—like one in four Americans—may be co-dependent. You may be dependent upon alcohol or drugs, money, work, food, or sexuality for happiness—or maybe you love someone who is."

Such persons are enduring life, rather than living it.

Even though we may not identify with any of the statements which suggest we are codependent and/or addictive, don't we feel ourselves at times feeling forced to endure life rather than live it? And what most often makes us feel that way is our drivenness to be good by loving and caring for someone else.

Yesterday I shared the story of my mother. There is a lot of my mother in me. Being an ordained minister, a *professional care-er,* intensifies the possibility of my loving and caring being distorted. One of the most difficult lessons I have had to learn is that every need is not a call. Every call for help does not necessarily have my name on it.

Frequently I get bogged down in caring and doing good to the point that I feel I am a robot, enduring life, but not really living it—not choosing to love, not being a servant out of compassion that reflects the love of Jesus flowing through me. We will deal more with this in Week Seven. For now, let's focus our reflections.

Reflecting and Recording

Spend some time reflecting on this thought: *not every need is a call, and not every call has my name on it.*

Are you experiencing present pressures because you are seeking to respond to needs you simply cannot meet? Make some notes here, naming these needs and pressures.

Offer a prayer of surrender of yourself and these needs to the Lord.

During the Day

Pay attention to how you move through this day. Are you choosing to live, love, care—or, are you enduring life?

Day Six

HOW DO YOU DIVIDE THE PIE?

OUR LIFE IS LIVED IN SEGMENTS (as suggested by the authors of *Love Is a Choice*), divided according to the various roles we play and the time and energy we devote to different calls on us. Below is an "unsliced" pie. Let the pie represent your life. How do you divide it? In my own life, preparing sermons and preaching represents a much larger slice than my hobby, attending auctions or estate sales. Being a mother of three children under ten would represent for a mother a far larger slice than playing bridge.

Look at the circle below; see it as a pie. Divide the pie to represent your life. One wedge may be job. Others may be marriage, family, friends, church, recreation, hobbies, time alone, or other designations for a portion of your life.

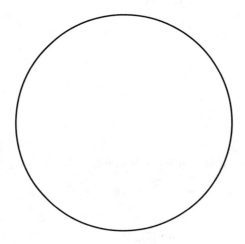

The doctors of the Minirth-Meier Clinic remind us that: "A healthy person's pie chart will consist of many wedges, and although they are of different sizes, all more or less [are] in balance with one another" (Hemfelt, Minirth, Meier, p. 133).

Here is the factor we need to deal with as we face the issue of codependency or the possibility that *being good may be bad for us.*

The codependent's chart will appear distorted, particularly if the wedges represent the amount of emotional energy spent on the various roles. In terms of emotional effort, the codependent is so obsessed with one overbearing relationship that every other wedge shrinks. There are just so many hours in a day, just so many ergs of available energy. The codependent squanders huge blocks of time and energy dealing with one person and that one person's problems. With one thing absorbing so much of the codependent's focus, precious little time and energy remain to be focused upon the other wedges.

Now you can see graphically why a child receives nurturance from less-than-one-parent if one parent is "clean" and the other enslaved to alcohol, drugs, or a severe compulsion. The nonaddict is preoccupied, feeling guilty, feeling resentful, hurt, attempting to handle crises—in short, absorbed in that problematic other person. No matter how loved, the child has become a very small wedge in the parent's pie.

Commonly in malignant codependent relationships, the first to go are friendships. Church relationships flounder. Even if other slices still exist, they're squeezed down to a small area of total energy expended and attention given.

Medical biology provides an illustration with tumors. The tumor itself may not be malignant. But as it grows, feeding on the host energy, it crowds out the healthy tissue. The tumor itself we could live with, but the crowding and loss of healthy tissue threaten life. Look at the codependent, by partial analogy, as a person inflicted with just such an emotional tumor. The problem relationship crowds out the healthy relationships and activities that would bring balance and richness to life. (Hemfelt, Minirth and Meier, pp. 133–134)

Reflecting and Recording

Look now at the way you divided your pie. Where are you spending most of your time?

Who or what is getting your attention?

Are persons who need and deserve your care and attention not getting it because you are investing too much somewhere else?

In the way you divide your pie, can you see signals of your being good being bad for you?

During the Day

The Apostle Paul reminds us to "let your love be genuine." Think about that call throughout the day as you interact with others.

Day Seven

GET REAL

Consider the incredible love that the Father has shown us in allowing us to be called "children of God"—and that is not just what we are called, but what we *are*. This explains why the world will no more recognize us than it recognized Christ.

Here and now, my dear friends, we are God's children. We don't know what we shall become in the future. We only know that when he appears we shall be like him, for we shall see him as he is!

—1 John 3:1-2, PHILLIPS

IN A CARTOON, ZIGGY IS LOOKING at a greeting card display. One section is labeled "Get Well"; the other, "Get Real." That's our need. We're not going to get well until we get real. Many of us are not well because we have given in to codependency. Our addiction is "helping others," but too often our help doesn't really help.

As Christians we are called to "love one another," to serve one another, and to give ourselves to and for others. But as Bob Olmstead reminds us, "That does not mean covering up for others, doing for others what those others need to do for themselves. It does not mean helping others maintain lies and addictions. Love and truth are not incompatible."

If we are going to break the cycle of being good in a way that may be bad for us, we must get real. Getting real calls first for honesty. The first principle of recovery, of health and wholeness, is truth. One cannot begin the twelve steps of Alcoholics Anonymous until he or she says, out loud, in public, "I'm an alcoholic."

On Days Four and Five, we looked at the possibility that being good is bad for us when we compulsively care for others and ignore caring for ourselves, and when our caring for others forces us to endure life, rather than to live it. We need to be honest in facing up to these possibilities in our lives.

As Christians we may find ourselves in a bind. What selfless, sacrificial love requires is not always clear in most situations. Some directions can be ours if we will seek to "get real." These directions flow from what we have considered on previous pages. One, stop enduring life and begin to live it; and, two, cease compulsively caring for others and begin to care for ourselves.

Overarching everything else is this: God's unconditional love for us is the answer to our hunger for love. Most of our dysfunction, our failure in wholeness, stems from a self-perception that we are unloved and unlovable. Another destructive self-perception is that we are responsible for others' pain and suffering.

The reversal of this destructive self-perception requires something like a conversion. Others may help facilitate the process for us, but ultimately it's an inside job, something we must claim and experience. It's a choice: to receive the love of God which already has been given, and begin the long process of coloring our whole life with that reality.

Reflecting and Recording

Our being loved by God is an undergirding truth of this workbook. We will return to it often. For now, go back and read 1 John 3:1-2, printed at the beginning of this session.

Spend some time letting the truth sink in: "We are God's children" now—incredible love!

Move in your mind back over the week. You may want to review the workbook content of the week and recall some of your reactions and responses. Then write a brief prayer, expressing your feelings.

If you are in a sharing group, make your plans to attend the meeting this week.

During the Day

Find three or four times during the day to sing aloud or silently in your mind the children's song that expresses a wondrous truth adults need to accept.

Jesus loves me! This I know, for the Bible tells me so.
Little ones to him belong, they are weak, but he is strong.

Yes, Jesus loves me! Yes, Jesus loves me!
Yes, Jesus loves me! The Bible tells me so.

GROUP MEETING FOR WEEK TWO

Introduction

Participation in a group such as this is a covenant relationship. You will profit most as you keep the daily discipline of the thirty-minute period and as you faithfully attend these weekly meetings.

Our growth, in part, hinges upon our group participation, so share as openly and honestly as you can. Listen to what persons are saying. Sometimes there is meaning beyond the surface of their words which you may pick up if you are really attentive.

Being a sensitive participant in this fashion is crucial. Responding immediately to the feelings we pick up is also crucial. Sometimes it is important for the group to focus its entire attention on a particular individual. If some need or concern is expressed, it may be appropriate for the leader to ask the group to enter into a brief period of special prayer for the persons or concerns revealed. Participants should not always depend upon the leader for this kind of sensitivity, for the leader may miss it. Even if you aren't the leader, don't hesitate to ask the group to join you in special prayer.

Remember, you have a contribution to make to the group. What you consider trivial or unimportant may be just what another person needs to hear. We are not seeking to be profound but simply to share our experience.

Sharing Together

Note: It will not be possible in this time frame to use all these suggestions. The leader should select what will be most beneficial to the group. It is important that the leader be thoroughly familiar with these suggestions in order to move through them *selectively* according to the direction in which the group is moving and according to the time available. The leader should plan ahead, but do not hesitate to change your plan according to the nature of the sharing taking place and the needs that emerge.

1. Open your time together with the leader offering a brief prayer of thanksgiving for the opportunity of sharing with the group and petitions for openness in sharing and loving response to each other.

2. In your "Reflecting and Recording" period on Day Two you were asked to check the statement or statements about codependents that describe you, and to underline specific words or phrases that say something about how you respond to others and circumstances. Invite as many persons as will to share their responses, describing relationships and experiences of those ways of relating.

Don't rush this sharing. It will help the group appropriate the meaning of codependency.

3. Spend ten minutes talking about the negative aspects of love seeking to control. Don't talk in theory or abstractly, but how you have experienced love being used to control.

4. There may be a person in the group who grew up in a home with an alcoholic or other drug-addicted parent—or is presently a part of a family in which a member is an addict. If it is not a violation of confidence, and that person (or persons) is free to share, it would be helpful for that person to talk about what it is like to live in such a relationship. Give special attention to how other members of the family help the addict "maintain his or her lie."

5. Invite one or two persons to share the story of someone who compulsively covers for others, but ignores caring for himself or herself.

6. Spend the balance of your time with persons sharing new insights that have come to them this week; how, and to what degree, have they discovered themselves to be codependent? Keep pressing the question: Is "helping others" an addiction?

Praying Together

As stated last week, the effectiveness of this group and the quality of relationship will be enhanced by a commitment to pray for each other by name each day. If you have pictures of each other, as requested last week, put these pictures face down on a table and let each person select a picture. This person will be the focus of special prayer for the week. Bring the photos back next week, shuffle them, and draw again. Continue this throughout your pilgrimage together. Looking at a person's picture as you pray for that person will add meaning. Having the picture will also remind you that you are to give special prayer attention to this person during the week.

1. Praying corporately each week is a special ministry. Take some time now for a period of verbal prayer, allowing each person to mention any special needs he or she wishes to share with the entire group.

A good pattern is to ask for a period of prayer after each need is mentioned. There may be silent prayer by the entire group, or someone may offer a brief two- or three-minute verbal sentence prayer.

2. Close your time by praying together the great prayer of the church, "Our Father." As you pray this prayer, remember that you are linking yourselves with all Christians of all time in universal intercession.

WEEK THREE

Growing in Self-esteem

YOU ARE MORE THAN YOU THINK YOU ARE

THE BACK DOOR SLAMMED AND THE LITTLE BOY CAME INTO THE KITCHEN, threw his baseball down on the floor, and stood there on the verge of tears. "What in the world is the matter?" his mother asked. "Did you lose the game?"

"Worse than that," the little fellow sobbed. "I was traded."
"Now, now. That's all part of the game. Sometimes even the world's greatest baseball stars are traded. Why should being traded upset you so?"

"Because," the little boy said, "I was traded for Harry's six-year-old sister."

Negative and positive things happen throughout life to build our self-esteem or to rob us of it. This is one of the biggest issues in life. I doubt if any reader has not had to deal with it in one way or another.

Let's begin our consideration of this issue with this needful recognition: One of the greatest tragedies is to die without knowing who you are. Or, you can put it this way: One of the greatest tragedies is to live denying who you are.

Can you believe me when I tell you, "You are more than you think you are"? I can ask the question honestly because it took me a long time to believe it for myself. For a good part of my life I spent a huge amount of energy trying to prove myself worthy of love and acceptance. My low estimate of myself set the agenda for my ceaseless efforts to be accepted.

I grew up in poverty in rural Mississippi. Despite the sacrificial love and the total commitment of my parents to my well-being, I allowed what I perceived as my cultural, social, economic and educational deprivation to distort reality and shape my self-image. In my rebellion against this background, I have spent a good part of my life *proving* myself to others. My game has been: "*See here, I am worthy of your love and acceptance."* I have been a slavish worker, tirelessly bent on achieving and performing. I have driven myself mercilessly to success, a fear of failure constantly drawing from me more and more energy, and serving as the demanding taskmaster of my life. I could not bear the threat of failure, whatever my activity.

I have spent massive energy in unproductive efforts, including the building of stages on which to perform. This was my neurotic effort to prove myself to others—a desire to be accepted by them.

Along the way, and I'll share more about this as we move along this workbook journey, I experienced a conversion other than my initial conversion to Christ. This conversion came slowly and painfully. But it came, hallelujah, it came! The awareness pervaded the total perspective of my life: "I am more than I thought I was."

Psalm 8 became a part of my view of reality.

> When I look at your heavens, the work of your fingers,
> the moon and the stars that you have established;
> what are human beings that you are mindful of them?
> Yet you have made them a little lower than God,
> and crowned them with glory and honor.
> You have given them dominion over the works of your hands;
> you have put all things under their feet.
>   —Psalm 8:3-6

The message got through. I am a creation of God, thus of infinite worth. I am loved by God, and there are other persons who love me, therefore I don't have to prove myself. My struggle for self-esteem was energized and brought into perspective.

Reflecting and Recording

Spend some time looking at your life, reflecting on your experience with the issue of self-esteem.

During the Day

Memorize this affirmation:

Dear God, you have made me a little lower than yourself, and crowned me with glory and honor.
Repeat that affirmation throughout the day.

Day Two

SHAPED BY FORCES WE DON'T CONTROL

CHARLES H. COOLEY IS AN IMPORTANT MODERN SOCIAL SCIENTIST, and is considered the dean of American sociology. He developed the concept of the "looking-glass self." Persons who have taken even an elementary course in sociology have been introduced to this concept of human understanding. Cooley's theory goes like this: A person's self-concept is established by what he or she thinks the most important persons in his or her life think of him or her. Get that. Our self-image is shaped by what we think the most important persons in our life think of us.

Well, who are the most important persons in our life at the time when our identity is being formed, our self-image shaped? Our family: mothers, fathers, siblings, and our closest friends.

What I want to say now is not designed to make anyone's guilt more pronounced, but to give us a perspective on how we come to be as we are; also to give us direction for relating to others—especially to little ones.

What others said "you are" when we were children, to a marked degree becomes the "I am" as we grow older and claim our identity. David Seamands made it more specific in *Healing Grace:*

> The perceived "You are's" of the parents become the inner "I am's" of the children. I do not want to limit this to parents or step-parents, because other family members, neighbors, peers, teachers, and church personnel also play a major role. However, there is no doubt parents are the main ones involved. It is not that they necessarily word their rejection and

say, "You are this" or "You are that." The message is given by their overall personalities, their inner and outer bearing and demeanor, by the radar they send out." (Seamands, *Healing Grace*, p. 153)

Seamands provides a long list of the put-downs children receive, many of them coming from their parents. Here are some samples of the "You are's" which easily become "I am's."

You've no right to feel that way.
If you can't say something nice, don't say anything.
Why do you always do things like that?
If there's a wrong way to do it, you'll find it.
What makes you so stupid? clumsy? dumb? slow? silly?
All you gotta' do is use your head once in a while.
I can't believe you did such a thing. (Seamands, p. 154)

Do you see it? The "You are's" become the "I am's" because we accept the image imposed on us by the people who mean the most to us.

This kind of shaping another person's self-image becomes a "pain that never goes away."

There are other forces we do not control that shape us. I shared yesterday the shaping power of what I perceived to be my cultural, social, economic, and educational deprivation. To recognize these factors and to deal with them honestly is part of the movement toward self-esteem.

Reflecting and Recording

Read again the sample listing of "You are's" which easily become "I am's." Put a check (√) by any that you remember having been spoken to you, or something like it.

Write as many other statements as you can recall, spoken to you as a child, which you accepted as describing who you are ("you are's" that became "I am's" for you).

Growth in self-esteem comes only as we change our perception of ourselves. The Christian faith will shape our self-perception if we will allow it to do so. Let the following scripture speak to you.

Consider the incredible love that the Father has shown us in allowing us to be called "children of God"—and that is not just what we are called, but what we *are*. This explains why the world will no more recognize us than it recognized Christ.

Here and now, my dear friends, we *are* God's children. We don't know what we shall become in the future. We only know that when he appears we shall be like him, for we shall see him as he is!

—1 John 3:1-3, Phillips

During the Day

Continue using the affirmation,

Dear God, you have made me a little lower than yourself, and crowned me with glory and honor.

Day Three

IF WE THINK WE ARE NOTHING, WE WILL LIVE AND ACT AS THOUGH WE WERE NOTHING

I have heard of your faith in the Lord Jesus and your love toward all the saints, and for this reason I do not cease to give thanks for you as I remember you in my prayers. I pray that the God of our Lord Jesus Christ, the Father of glory, may give you a spirit of wisdom and revelation as you come to know him, so that, with the eyes of your heart enlightened, you may know what is the hope to which he has called you, what are the riches of his glorious inheritance among the saints, and what is the immeasurable greatness of his power for us who believe, according to the working of his great power. God put this power to work in Christ when he raised him from the dead and seated him at his right hand in the heavenly places.

—Ephesians 1:15–20

I ONCE HEARD A POPULAR TALK SHOW HOST say a very insightful thing on a TV show. "My life seems like one long obstacle course, with me as the chief obstacle."

Do you feel that way sometimes—that life is an obstacle course and that you are the chief obstacle, in living life to the fullest, as God would have it, and as Christ offers it?

The truth is this: *If we think we are nothing we will live and act as though we were nothing.* The above passage from Ephesians has this attention-getting phrase: *the eyes of your heart.* Isn't it true? We see ourselves from the very depths of our personality. Thus, as David Seamands reminds us, "When we see ourselves from the perceptive of destructive *"I am's,"* then our self-esteem is affected from the very center of our being" (Seamands, p. 157).

A friend of mine witnesses to this.

As a child, she recognized that she wasn't as smart as one of her younger sisters or as pretty as the other. She had to prove herself in some way, and so she assumed the characteristic of being "strong." When other people went to pieces, she stood as solid as a rock. People could bring their problems and pour them into her ears. Her parents, sisters, other relatives, and friends encouraged this stance. The expression that she remembers most clearly from childhood and youth is, "Marj is the strong one!"

Marj carried this image of strength over into her marriage and parenthood. Now, at age fifty, she is discovering the joy that can come with being accepted despite her weakness. In church groups, she has been able to fail and acknowledge failure. "Marj is the strong one" no longer haunts her and drives her to phoniness. Her marriage has found new life. Her husband, who fell into the snare of expecting perfection from her, has blossomed in his personhood because she is now evoking his gifts of strength and creativity, whereas before she had smothered him.

Reflecting and Recording

My friend Marj got boxed into acting always as the "strong one." She saw herself through "the eyes of her heart" because that image had been firmly planted there by those she loved.

How do you see yourself through "the eyes of your heart"? List three dominant images:

———————————————

———————————————

———————————————

Now look at each of those images and write beside each image the name of the persons or circumstances that shaped it.

Spend some time thinking about how these images affect your self-esteem.

During the Day

Pay attention to the way you respond to others throughout the day. Do any responses flow out of low self-esteem? Remember, if you think you are nothing, you will live and act as though you were nothing.

Day Four

THERE IS SOMETHING WE CAN BE BUT WILL NEVER BE APART FROM JESUS CHRIST

ON DAY TWO, WE CONSIDERED DR. COOLEY'S CONCEPT of the "looking-glass self." A person's self-concept is established by what he or she thinks the most important person in his or her life thinks of him or her.

Here is where Christians must center. Though essential, it's not enough to believe that we are created and loved by God and that God doesn't want us to live a mediocre life. Low self-esteem, self-devaluation, and self-hate may continue after we believe that—even after we become Christians, maybe even long after we become Christians. For many the personality damages have been so great, the forces that have shaped our self-image have done such a destructive job that conversion to Christ is not enough to overcome the grip these notions of worthlessness have on us.

The grip is sometimes so great that we feel that God, also, disapproves of us and thinks we are nothing. "The first step in our healing is to realize that God understands where the feelings are coming from and is as brokenhearted about it as we are. He wants to work with us in freeing us from them, for He doesn't want His children despising themselves. Truly our only hope is a whole new way of viewing ourselves through the eyes of grace" (Seamands, *Healing Grace*, p. 157). And those eyes of grace center on Jesus Christ. There is something we can be but will never be apart from Jesus Christ.

As Christians the most important person in our lives is Jesus. Therefore, our self-concept may and can be established by what he thinks of us.

> See what love the Father has given us, that we should be called
> children of God; and that is what we are. The reason the world
> does not know us is that it did not know him.

Beloved, we are God's children now; what we will be has not yet been revealed. What we do know is this: when he is revealed, we will be like him, for we will see him as he is.

—1 John 3:1-2

What does Jesus think of us? He loves us as though we were the only person in the world to love. He loves you so much that he died for you. The cross would have happened if you were the only one who would receive grace. That's what Jesus thinks of you.

In his book, *The Sensation of Being Somebody*, Maurice E. Wagner reminds us of the three essential components of a healthy self-image. One, *a sense of belongingness*, of being loved. Two, *a sense of worth and value*. Three, *a sense of being competent*. As already indicated, our self-image comes from many sources—some of these forces we have no control over.

We have no control over the physical, emotional, and spiritual equipment with which we are born. That is, we came into the world with senses, a capacity to learn, and certain physical characteristics. What we do not control is *given* at birth. This may include limitations, handicaps, and deformities. There is a sense in which this is our *inner* world.

As we do not control this inner world, this *given* at birth, so we do not control much of our outer world. We focused on this on Day Two: our parents, family, friends; those who feed us with the "you are's" that become the destructive "I am's."

The inner and outer forces we have no control over play a star role in our sense of belongingness, of worth and value, of being competent. Blessed indeed are those who have significant others who love, accept, forgive, support, and affirm them into a healthy self-image. At best, however, these are limited. We need Jesus Christ. There is something we can be, but will never be apart from him.

Consider Jesus' relation to the three essential components of a healthy self-image.

A sense of belongingness, of being loved. One of the incredible dimensions of the Christian faith is that we belong to Christ. We abide in Him. He dwells in us. Listen to Jesus:

Abide in me as I abide in you. Just as the branch cannot bear fruit by itself unless it abides in the vine, neither can you unless you abide in me. I am the vine, you are the branches. Those who abide in me and I in them bear much fruit, because apart from me you can do nothing. . . . As the Father has loved me, so I have loved you; abide in my love.

—John 15:4–5, 9

A sense of worth and value. We have to know that we count, that we are of value. Can we believe it—that Jesus values us so much that he would die for us?

Those who have been born of God do not sin, because God's seed abides in them; they cannot sin, because they have been born of God. The children of God and the children of the devil are revealed in this way: all who do not do what is right are not from God, nor are those who do not love their brothers and sisters.

—1 John 3:9–10

A sense of being competent. What power Jesus adds here! Can we say with Paul, "I can do all things through him [Christ] who strengthens me" (Phil. 4:13)?

Reflecting and Recording

Consider your relationship to Jesus Christ. What is that relationship doing for your sense of belongingness, of being loved? Your sense of worth and value? Are you allowing that relationship to enhance your sense of being competent?

Write a couple of paragraphs expressing your reflections and feelings.

During the Day

Pray this prayer throughout the day: "Oh God, help me to believe the truth about myself, no matter how beautiful it is."

Day Five

LET GOD PAINT THE PORTRAIT

IN *THE BROTHERS KARAMAZOV*, Dostoevski characterized the artificial life of the monastery as "twenty-five men trying to be saints, who sit around looking blankly at each other and eat cabbage."

Helen Keller said, "There is no king who has not had a slave among his ancestors, and no slave who has not had a king among his."

We human beings are a mixture and a mess of the earth and of heaven; sinners, yes, but created "a little less than God." We inherit a blend of dignity and degradation. All of us, but addicts and codependents to a far greater and destructive degree, feel ashamed of what we do, even of who we are. In fact, our shame often overwhelms us.

We want to fix things. Our oversensitivity to our sin, failure, flaws, and shame puts us in a kind of competition with God. We want to diagnose and prescribe the cure. We will not allow ourselves to be human, nor will we allow God to be God. *Self-esteem flourishes when we let God paint the portrait.*

Growth in self-esteem involves choice:
- Whether we will continue in those "boxes" in which we have been placed;
- living as those "images" created by persons who may have loved us but sinned terribly against us by making us feel like nothing,
- being victims of the handicaps, limitations, deformities that were *given* at birth;
- or, whether we will let God paint the portrait.

Some questions suggested by David Seamands will help us get a vision of the portrait.

• What right have you to belittle or despise someone whom God *loves* so deeply? Don't say, "Well, I know God loves me, but I just can't stand myself." That's a travesty of faith, an insult to God and His love. It is the expression of a subtly hidden resentment against your Creator. When you despise His creation, you are really saying that you don't like the design or care much for the Designer. You are calling unclean what God calls clean. You are failing to realize how much God loves you and how much you mean to Him.

• What right have you to belittle or despise someone whom God has *honored* so highly? "Consider the incredible love that the Father has shown us in allowing us to be called 'children of God'" (1 John 3:1, PH). And that's not just what we're called. It's what we are. "Oh, dear children of mine . . . have you realized it? Here and now we are God's children" (v. 2, PH).

Do you think that when you consider God's son or daughter worthless or inferior, He is pleased by your so-called humility?

• What right have you to belittle or despise someone whom God *values* so highly? How much does God value you? "In human experience it is a rare thing for one man to give his life for another, even if the latter be a good man. . . . Yet the proof of God's amazing love is this: that it was while we were sinners that Christ died for us. . . . We may hold our heads high in the light of God's love" (Rom. 5:7-8, 11, PH). God has declared your value. You are someone whom God values so highly as to give the life of His own dear Son to redeem you.

• What right have you to belittle or despise someone whom God has *provided* for so fully? "How much more shall your Father which is in heaven give good things?" (Matt. 7:11) "God shall supply all your need" (Phil. 4:19). This doesn't sound as if He wants you to be self-loathing or to feel inadequate.

• What right have you to belittle or despise someone whom God has *planned* for so carefully?

Praise be to God. . . . for giving us through Christ every spiritual benefit. . . . Consider what He has done—before the foundation of the world He chose us to become in Christ, His holy and blameless children, living within His constant care. He planned, in His purposeful love, that we should be adopted as His own children (Eph. 1:3-5, PH).

• What right have you to belittle or despise someone in whom God *delights?* The Apostle Paul said that we are "accepted in the beloved" (Eph. 1:6). Do you remember the Father's words at the baptism of Jesus? "This is My beloved Son in whom I am well pleased" (Seamands, *Healing Damaged Emotions*, pp. 73-74).

Reflecting and Recording

Spend a few minutes reflecting on these questions: Have you listened to God's opinion of you? Have you let God paint your portrait?

To give explicit expression to your reflections, fill in the chart below. In the left column, "I see myself," list the negative ways you see yourself or feelings you have about yourself; i.e., "unworthy of love." List as many as you can up to five. Then continue in the left column with the positive feelings or ways you see yourself. Do that now.

I SEE MYSELF	GOD SEES ME
Negative	1.
1.	2.
2.	3.
3.	4.
4.	5.
5.	6.
Positive	7.
1.	8.
2.	9.
3.	10.
4.	11.
5.	12.

Now, make a list of the ways God sees you and feels about you. You may want to review the above questions suggested by Seamands.

Now, offer a prayer of thanksgiving to God, and make a commitment to seek to live according to God's portrait of you.

During the Day

If you are sharing this workbook with a group, select one person in the group to call by phone today, or to visit personally, and share your feelings and responses to this week's focus on self-esteem.

Call or write some person not in the group and share the prayer you have been praying: "Oh God, help me to believe the truth about myself, no matter how beautiful it is." You may want to select someone whom you think really needs to pray that prayer.

Day Six

LOCATE AND FACE THE CHIEF SOURCES
OF YOUR LOW SELF-ESTEEM

Today and tomorrow we will look at some practical suggestions for dealing with and overcoming our low self-esteem. I am aware that what I am suggesting here is not something you will accomplish today or tomorrow. I'm talking about a process.

You may also need help—a pastor, a trusted friend, your sponsor if you are in a Twelve-Step Program, or a professional counselor. I'm simply pointing the way and inviting you to walk in it with a trusted guide or companion.

The first is this: Locate and face the painful places, persons, and experiences of your past which you feel are the chief sources of your low self-esteem.

Now we don't do this in order to blame others or to evade our own responsibilities. We do it in order that we might honestly face up to our feelings—feelings that we may have kept buried for years.

Someone has described the Twelve Steps of Alcoholics Anonymous as "the biggest healing gift of the twentieth century." Whether the "biggest" or not, these steps are a precious gift and provide a very effective guide for healing and wholeness.

Step Four calls us to locate and face the chief sources of our low self-esteem: "Made a searching and fearless moral inventory of ourselves." This call comes to us in many ways in scripture. A consummate expression of it is Lamentations 3:40: "Let us test and examine our ways, and return to the Lord."

With Step Four and continuing through Step Seven, we have a forceful guide for self-discovery and healing:

4. Made a searching and fearless moral inventory of ourselves.
5. Admitted to God, to ourselves, and to another human being, the exact nature of our wrongs.
6. Were entirely ready to have God remove all these defects of character.
7. Humbly asked Him to remove our shortcomings.

As indicated in our discussion of codependency last week, most of us are involved in addictive behavior. Yet, we do not have to be addicts, as commonly understood, to use and benefit from these steps. They help us get in touch with our "shadow," that part of ourselves that we have suppressed and kept hidden, but which works mightily to keep us bound in feelings of worthlessness. It is these hidden experiences and feelings which are major blocks to God and barriers to self-esteem.

Bill Wilson in the *Big Book* of Alcoholics Anonymous helps us locate and face these painful places, persons, and experiences of our past by guiding us to look at three categories: resentments, fears, and harms done to others. The first two, resentments and fears, are chief sources of our low self-esteem.

Think about it. To identify resentment toward people, places, and things which have injured us gets us in touch with forces that have shaped us, that have made us feel shameful and worthless. To identify our fears also helps us deal with the root of other repressive and painful feelings. Let's experiment, responding to the scriptural call, "Let us test and examine our ways, and return to the Lord."

Reflecting and Recording

I'm indebted to Joe McQ. of "The Big Book Study Tapes" in *The Steps We Took* (August House Publishers, Inc., Little Rock, 1990) for this suggested exercise.

Complete column one before you do anything in column two. In column one, list persons, places, institutions, or experiences at which you are resentful.

COLUMN ONE I'm Resentful At:	COLUMN TWO The Cause:
1.	
2.	
3.	
4.	
5.	

Now go back to each resentment listing and ask, "What made me angry? Why am I resentful?" Make notes in column two—The Cause.

Do the same thing now with your fears, filling out the first column completely before you seek to name "the cause."

COLUMN ONE I'm Fearful of:	COLUMN TWO Why Do I Have the Fear?
1.	
2.	
3.	
4.	
5.	

Tomorrow, we will deal with the issue of forgiveness as a source of healing and wholeness. Close your time with a prayer, offering to God these exercises as your confession of who you are and the pain you feel.

During the Day

As indicated earlier, this is only a suggestion of a process. You may want to think about ways to continue the process, and take specific steps such as sharing with your pastor or a trusted friend.

Did you call someone and share the prayer you've been praying ("Oh God, help me to believe the truth about myself, no matter how beautiful it is.")? Why not call another person today for whom the prayer might be meaningful.

> Day Seven

DAILY COOPERATION WITH CHRIST

YESTERDAY I SUGGESTED THAT A FIRST STEP in dealing with and overcoming our low self-esteem is to locate and face the painful places, persons, and experiences of our past which we feel are the chief sources of our lack of self-esteem. Today we consider two other practical suggestions.

One, *as you face the pain of past experiences, forgive everyone involved.* Jesus spoke to this issue in his Sermon on the Mount.

> So when you are offering your gift at the altar, if you remember that your brother or sister has something against you, leave your gift there before the altar and go; first be reconciled to your brother or sister, and then come and offer your gift.
>
> —Matthew 5:23-24

Resentment and fear are chains that keep us bound to the people and pains of the past. Only forgiveness and love can free us, can release us from resentment and fear. Without forgiveness, resentment and fear will hinder and undermine our growth in overcoming shame and developing a sense of value and worthiness.

We must forgive those who have hurt us and seek the forgiveness of those we have hurt. We will deal more with this in Week Five.

The second suggestion is this: Commit yourself to daily cooperation with Christ to give you a renewed self-image. There is something you can be but will never be apart from Jesus Christ, and that takes hard work. Transformation is rarely instantaneous and/or easy. It involves the tough process of renewing the mind. That involves forgiving those who have wronged and hurt us in the past—but also forgiving ourselves and refusing to continue flagellating ourselves for past sins.

Consider John's words again.

See what love the Father has given us, that we should be called the children of God; and that is what we are. . . . Beloved, we are God's children now; what we will be has not yet been revealed. What we do know is this: when he is revealed, we will be like him, for we will see him as he is.

—1 John 3:1-2

Healing grace is not simply a one-time crisis gift. It may begin in a flash of insight or a very emotional high when we experience God's love and grace at a new and deeper level. *I would never belittle these spiritual highs in any way.* However, because emotions have been *badly overemphasized* in some Christian quarters, many pastors and counselors tend to *badly underemphasize* their importance. There are times when it takes a profoundly emotional experience to move a person off dead center, to loosen the mind from former mistaken perceptions, and *to actually free the will to make new decisions.* I have seen God work this way in many lives.

However, even when it *starts* that way, there is still the hard work of transformation by the renewal of the mind. Old internal *put-down I am's* are hard to break. A daily, moment-by-moment cooperation with the *instant counter-activity of the Holy Spirit is essential.* When I recently had knee surgery, I learned that the operation was only *half of the healing.* Faithfully doing the exercises given me by the physical therapist *was the equally important other half.* The same is true in the therapeutic exercises following a dynamic experience of healing grace. (Seamands, *Healing Grace,* pp. 164–165)

Reflecting and Recording

Go back to your reflecting and recording exercise yesterday. Look at every source or cause of resentment and fear. In every instance where it is needed, pray for forgiveness, or forgive those who have brought you pain.

♥

During the Day

If there is any person on your list of causes for resentment and fear whom you need to speak to—asking forgiveness or offering yours—call that person by phone or write a letter today.

If you are in a group which will be meeting today, pray before you go—that your time together will be a source of affirmation and self-esteem for every person.

GROUP MEETING FOR WEEK THREE

Note: The leader for this week should bring a chalkboard or newsprint to the group meeting. See suggestion 1 of "Sharing Together."

Introduction

Two essential ingredients of a Christian fellowship are *feedback* and *follow-up.* Feedback is necessary to keep the group dynamic working positively for all participants. Follow-up is essential to express Christian concern and ministry.

The leader is primarily responsible for feedback in the group. All persons should be encouraged to share their feeling about how the group is functioning. Listening is crucial. To listen to another, as much as any other action, is a means of affirming that person. When we listen to another, we are saying, "You are important; I value you." It is also crucial to check out meaning in order that those who are sharing the pilgrimage may know that we really hear. We often miss-hear. "Are you saying ____?" is a good check question. It takes only a couple of persons in a group, who listen and give feedback in this fashion, to set the mood for the group.

Follow-up is the function of everybody. If we listen to what others are saying, we will discover needs and concerns beneath the surface, situations that deserve special prayer and attention. Make notes of these as the group shares. Follow up during the week with a telephone call, a written note of caring and encouragement, a visit. What distinguishes a Christian fellowship is *caring in action.* "My, how those Christians love one another!"

Our theme this week is "Growing in Self-Esteem." We grow as we are affirmed by others, so be sure to follow up each week with others in the group. Your ongoing expression of love will say, "You are important, you are worthy of attention and love."

Sharing Together

By this time, a significant amount of knowing each other exists in the group. Persons are feeling safe in the group, perhaps more willing to share. Still, there is no place for pressure. The leader, however, should be especially sensitive to those slow to share. Seek gently to coax them out. Every person is a gift to the group.

Listening and responding is important in building the self-esteem of another. When we really listen to another, we are saying, "You are important, I will hear and receive what you have to say." So, how we listen and respond to each other in these sharing sessions will be a contribution to growing in self-esteem.

1. Leader, copy this formula on chalkboard or newsprint: **OUR SELF-WORTH = PERFORMANCE + OTHERS' OPINIONS.**

Invite the group to think about this formula in silence for two minutes. Is it true? Do I act as though it is true?

2. In "popcorn" fashion ask persons to respond in only a sentence or two how they think other people would describe them. Let this be a spontaneous, quick sort of thing. Let as many persons share as want to before any other comments are made.

3. Now spend eight to ten minutes discussing the formula: "Our self-worth equals performance plus others' opinions." Do you believe it? Do you act as though you believe it?

4. Leader, copy this formula on a chalkboard or newsprint: **OUR SELF-WORTH = GOD'S TRUTH ABOUT US.**

Invite the group to think about this formula in silence for two minutes. Is it true? Do I act as though it is true? What is God's truth about me?

5. Ask persons to tell, in only a word or a sentence, their response to this question: "What is God's truth about us?" Write these on the chalkboard or newsprint, without comment from anyone, as they are spoken.

6. Now spend eight to ten minutes talking about the formula in relation to the previous one. Which do we really believe? Which do we live by?

7. Leader, have someone read aloud to the group the questions from David Seamands on Day Five.

Compare your list of "God's truth about us" with what is suggested about God's assessment of us. Can we agree on these as God's truth about us?

• God created and loves us. We are, therefore, special to God.

• Though we are sinners, God forgives. God sees us as children of potential and promise, and God's valuing of us is not dependent on our performance.

Take some time to discuss this.

8. Invite a couple of people to briefly share their story of how they adopted some destructive "I am's," and how their lives were shaped by what others thought of them.

9. On Day Four, we considered the fact that a sense of worth and value and a sense of being competent are essential for self-esteem. Invite two or three persons to share their experience of gaining those senses. Do Christ and the church play any role in providing that for us?

10. Discuss how persons in the group felt about the "Reflecting and Recording" exercise for Day Six.

Praying Together

1. The leader should take up the photographs of each group member, shuffle them, and let each person draw a new person to pray for.

2. Invite each member of the group to spend two minutes in quiet prayer for the person whose picture he or she had drawn, focusing on what the person has shared in this meeting.

3. Leader, ask the group if there are any special prayer requests. Are persons having difficulty facing some past experience and forgiving everyone involved? Is there someone in the group who does not feel loved and accepted by God? Is there need for healing of emotional wounds inflicted by those we love?

After special needs have been voiced, invite as many as will to pray aloud for those needs.

When the praying is finished, let the group stand, hold hands, and sing the children's song "Jesus Loves Me! This I Know."

Overcoming the Destructive Don'ts That Have Shaped Our Lives

YOU ARE KNOWN BY THE COMPANY YOU KEEP

FROM MY OWN EXPERIENCE OF WHOLENESS-SEEKING, desiring to be intentionally "under construction" as a Christian, I have discovered a fire smoldering inside me. Now and then it bursts into flames, and I have to deal with something I didn't even know was there. Unknown and unnamed guilt, hurt feelings never soothed and healed by the salve of recognition and attention, sin never confessed and forgiven, the labeling of me by others which unconsciously and without challenge I took as truth; and on it goes.

In my counseling ministry, I have discovered that this is a common dilemma. Even the most whole among us has to deal to some degree with a smoldering fire within. Some coals in this fire are the messages we received growing up.

. . . I'm no good.

. . . I'm not lovable.

. . . I'm clumsy.

. . . I'll never succeed.

Other coals are those feelings that were cultivated in us by persons we loved, or that came from sources we may never identify. We denied these feelings because they hurt too much to feel.

Our minds are full of ideas and notions that shape our lives; some of these are healthy, some unhealthy. That's the reason for our theme this week: *Overcoming the destructive don'ts that have shaped our lives.*

Through the years, from our parents and other people we have valued, from life itself, these destructive don'ts have been planted in our minds, and it's almost impossible not to keep company with them.

If I've heard it once, I've heard it hundreds of times—and so did most of you. It was one of my Mama's favorite exhortations. I think she thought it was a verse of scripture. She quoted it with that kind of authority: "A man is known by the company he keeps."

Was that ever said to you by your parents? Have you repeated it to your children? Maybe you think it is a verse of scripture also. It really isn't, but it is sound advice. A person is known by the company he or she keeps.

Thomas Bailey Aldrich has cast the truth differently. "A man is known by the company his mind keeps."

Now that isn't scripture either, but it's very close to it. Proverbs 23:7 puts it this way: "As he thinketh in his heart, so is he" (KJV). And Jesus said, "For out of the heart come evil intentions, murder, adultery, fornication, theft, false witness, slander" (Matt. 15:19).

Reflecting and Recording

Make a list of as many don'ts as you can recall that have been planted in your mind through the years. Don't judge them now, just write them down. Examples: "Don't take more food than you are going to eat," "Don't be angry," "Don't share your feelings."

Make your list now.

Now go back over the list. Don't spend a lot of time thinking about it, but put a checkmark (√) by those don'ts that may have served you well, and an "X" by those that may have had a negative effect.

During the Day

As you move through the day, try to determine whether your responses to others or situations are influenced by some "don't" that is a part of who you are.

Day Two

DON'T TRUST

"DO YOU HAVE TROUBLE HEARING?" asked the teacher of a youngster who sat dreamily at his desk.

"No, ma'am," replied the boy. "I have trouble listening."

That's a problem for many of us—listening. There is not only the problem of listening, there is the problem of listening *too much*. Or, put another way, most of us pay *too* much attention to the destructive don'ts of our life.

One of the most destructive is *don't trust*.

We've been taught not to trust. Maybe it has come to us in this way: "It's a dog-eat-dog world—you can't trust anyone." It doesn't help us to stop and think, "Have I ever known a dog to eat another dog?" The destructive don't is there: Don't trust.

I've heard it expressed this way: "I've been hurt before, and I'm never going to trust again." What is a little hurt when it comes to relationships? We can learn from pain. Leo Buscaglia explains it in his usual pungent way.

> What a silly world we live in, where you believe that everything has to be on a high, joyous level all the time. It kills me. We learn that from the media. We turn on our television sets and we see people giddy over cornflakes. They're absolutely freaking out! I saw an ad the other day that I couldn't believe. There was a woman—and I think it's degrading to womankind—she was going out of her mind over a new product called "A Thousand Flushes." Here she was in her toilet saying, "Oh, I love this product!" and "My life is complete!" (Buscaglia, p. 249)

Buscaglia concluded, "Good God, if your joy depends on 'A Thousand Flushes,' you're sick!"

We learn from pain. How much positive change and growth are we missing because of our fear of the pain which may come from a loving, trusting relationship? One of the things that all of us possess equally is our loneliness. Too many of us are willing to bear the pain of loneliness rather than risk the possible pain of trusting.

There is a marvelous proverb that teaches us, "Trust in the Lord with all your heart, and do not rely on your own insight" (Prov. 3:5). This is our most basic stance in relation to God—trust. As we can't have a meaningful relationship with God without trust, so with our interpersonal human relationships.

Reflecting and Recording

Were you taught not to trust? Reflect for a few minutes on the degree to which the message "don't trust" may have been destructive in some ways for you.

Our focus has been on trust in relationship to others. You may have been taught not to trust in other ways, such as "don't trust your feelings."

Make a list of the other "don't trust" messages you have received:

Don't trust _____.

Don't trust _____.

Don't trust _____.

Don't trust _____.

Don't trust _____.

Which of the above has been positive? Which negative?

In closing your time of reflection, think about your relationship to God through the years. Have there been times when you had difficulty trusting God?

During the Day

Pay attention to how the message, "don't trust," comes through in your attitudes, actions, and relationships today.

Day Three

DON'T BE VULNERABLE

HAVE YOU SEEN THE MOVIE OR READ THE BOOK *The Prince of Tides*? It's a revealing, penetrating commentary on life. It's really a secular sermon on "overcoming the destructive don'ts that have shaped our lives." Don't trust, don't risk, don't be vulnerable, were the lessons taught in widely different ways by the parents of Luke, Savannah, and Tom Wingo.

Savannah and Tom were the most pained victims. The most dramatic incident in the novel drove Savannah to the brink of insanity and to many suicide attempts, and shaped Tom into a person unable to love, to risk, to be vulnerable.

Their mother, Lila, refused to allow the father to be told or the police to be called about the devastating act of violence of which Lila, Savannah, and Tom were victims. The children and the mother never mentioned it again, never said a single word about it.

The mother forced them to keep the secret. Can you imagine going through life with that kind of secret—not speaking to your brother or your sister or your mother or anyone else about a destructive event that continues to ravage your life? The mother didn't want to run the risk, to be vulnerable, by allowing her husband and the community to know about that devastating experience.

Healing came to Tom, and began for Savannah, when they took that risk and became vulnerable and shared their life with each other and with the psychiatrist.

We can't live with destructive secrets. An old Ethiopian proverb says, "He who conceals his disease cannot expect to be cured." Somewhere along the way we must become vulnerable and run the risk of sharing.

Paul gives us a picture of the Christian church in this passage:

My friends, if anyone is detected in a transgression, you who have received the Spirit should restore such a one in a spirit of gentleness. Take care that you yourselves are not tempted. Bear one another's burdens, and in this way you will fulfill the law of Christ. For if those who are nothing think they are something, they deceive themselves.

—Galatians 6:1-3

It's a picture of sharing and caring. The fact is, there can be no caring apart from sharing. We may want to express our concern for another in action, but if we do not know what is going on in her life, then our expression of care will be limited.

Paul's direction is pointed: "Bear one another's burdens." Note the *mutuality*. This is not a one-way street. Contrary to the destructive "don't be vulnerable," or "guard your feelings," the journey to recovery involves mutual sharing, opening our lives to each other. A Swedish proverb says, "Shared joy is double joy, and shared sorrow is half-sorrow."

Our days are too long to carry grief alone and keep our joys to ourself.

The distinct dynamic of Twelve Step Recovery, whether Alcoholics Anonymous or other programs designed after this pattern, is vulnerability—the risk of telling *my* story. Members talk about their pain and unmanageable past lives, their spiritual experiences, their honest doubts and fears about themselves, and events of their daily life. This is a key element in healing and recovery.

Reflecting and Recording

In the very telling of our story, a degree of healing comes. Both Tom and Savannah experienced this in *The Prince of Tides*. It was only when they shared their pain, shame, guilt, anger, and resentment—only after becoming vulnerable enough to share their story with another that they began to recover from the devastating trauma and the *psychic numbing* that their mother's demand for secrecy had produced in them.

Is there a story you need to tell someone? Spend some time thinking about whether you may have been stunted in emotional and spiritual growth by adopting the destructive stance: guard your feelings, don't be vulnerable.

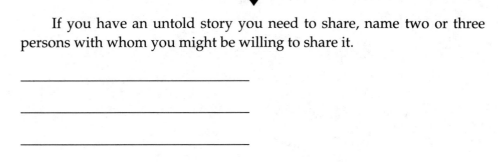

If you have an untold story you need to share, name two or three persons with whom you might be willing to share it.

_____

_____

_____

Pray for guidance in taking the next step.

During the Day

Be intentional today in putting the proverb to work: "Shared joy is double joy, and shared sorrow is half-sorrow." It doesn't have to be big and momentous things; the everyday experiences of joy and sorrow are to be shared.

Day Four

"DON'T BE SILLY"

WHAT COMES TO YOUR MIND WHEN YOU HEAR THE WORDS, "don't be silly"? Don't read any further; stop and think about occasions when you have heard those words, or when you may have spoken them.

Make some notes, describing your experience of having had those words spoken to you.

Now make some notes of *confession*—describing occasions when you have spoken those words to someone else.

I doubt if any reader has not heard that admonition. For many, it has been painful, even destructive. It has blunted our spontaneity. It has made us suspicious of fun and "lightness." It has turned some of us into slaves to *being proper*. It has robbed us of the joy of being ourselves. It has turned life into a serious competitive game in which we must never relax, never let down our guard, never reveal weakness, always be serious.

"Peanuts" is my favorite cartoon. In fact, "Peanuts" is among my favorite *everything*. Charles M. Schulz, the cartoonist, is a very perceptive and profound observer and commentator on life. In the first frame of a particular cartoon, Snoopy, "the hound of heaven," begins to wag his ears and leap about. "To dance is to live!" he says with gusto. In the next frame, he is twirling around, concluding to himself, "For me, dancing is an emotional outlet." In the third frame he says with deep feeling, "I feel sorry for people who can't dance." But, in the final frame, he goes leaping joyously away, admonishing us, "If you can't dance, you should at least be able to do a happy hop!"

It's a picture of Christians under construction and/or in recovery. We are overcoming the rigid boundaries on our ability to respond spontaneously, breaking the barriers to being flexible that were erected in our childhood and in what we have experienced in the past from persons and forces admonishing us, "don't be silly."

One of the tenderest stories coming out of World War II is that of a small English girl who prayed, "God, bless Mary and John, Joan and Michael, and, O God, take care of Yourself or we shall all be sunk." It illustrates the freedom of little children. Eric Marshall and Stuart Hample have done us a favor and provided laughter as well as instruction in what it's like to be alive as a little child in their collection of *Children's Letters to God.* (My favorite is "Dear God, I am sorry I was late for Sunday School, but I couldn't find my underwear. Norman.")

Children are open and alive. They have a perception that we adults seem to have lost. Best of all, they have what I call the capacity of LIVING LIGHTLY. They are not burdened down by preconceptions. Their lives are not predetermined by force of habit. They are not closed to others because of sour experiences. They don't keep grudges. They can *live lightly* because they don't have all the excess baggage we adults carry around. (Dunnam, p. 105)

No wonder Jesus said, "Unless you change and become like children" (Matt. 18:3). It may take us awhile to see the connection, but there is one—a connection between Jesus' call for us to become as little children, and his teaching in the Sermon on the Mount.

> Therefore I tell you, do not worry about your life, what you will eat or what you will drink, or about your body, what you will wear. Is not life more than food, and the body more than clothing? Look at the birds of the air; they neither sow nor reap nor gather into barns, and yet your heavenly Father feeds them. Are you not of more value than they?
>
> —Matthew 6:25-26

The two words that come to me as I consider this teaching of Jesus are *trust* and *surrender*. These are action/responses to life for the growing Christian. We deal with them in other ways throughout this workbook; for now, we focus on flexibility, on spontaneity. In our experiences of being told, "don't be silly," we had probably acted spontaneously, with no thought or regard about how others would perceive us or how foolish we might look. We were not guarding, or suppressing, the expression of our feelings. We didn't know it perhaps, but we were *expressing* and *responding*, rather than *controlling* and *reacting*. To whatever degree that we have lost it, we need to recover the capacity for spontaneity, for living lightly, even if it means "being silly."

Reflecting and Recording

Take a look at yourself by responding to these questions.

(1) Do I look for hidden meaning when the truth is on the surface?

(2) Do I look for and take on a battle when I could just as well let it pass and nothing would be lost?

(3) Do I suspect a person's motives when nothing is lost by taking him or her at face value?

(4) Do I give long explanations for my actions when none is called for?

How do these questions relate to the lesson we may have learned too well, "Don't be silly"?

♥

During the Day
Do at least one thing today that someone will think is silly.

Day Five

THE FINAL AMEN

THERE IS NO WAY FOR US TO EXAMINE EVERY DESTRUCTIVE DON'T. You made your own list in your "Reflecting and Recording" on Day One of this week. Since we can't consider each of these, I want to focus, in a general way, on overcoming these destructive don'ts.

Our direction is set by Paul in his Second Letter to the Corinthians.

> Do I make my plans according to ordinary human standards, ready to say "Yes, yes" and "No, no" at the same time? As surely as God is faithful, our word to you has not been "Yes and No." For the Son of God, Jesus Christ, whom we proclaimed among you, Silvanus and Timothy and I, was not "Yes and No"; but in him it is always "Yes."
> —2 Corinthians 1:17-19

Phillips translates verse 20:

> Every promise of God finds its affirmative in [Christ] and through him can be said the final amen, to the glory of God.

The setting for this word is enlightening. Paul is answering a criticism that had come to him from the Corinthians. They had accused him of being wishy-washy, of vacillating. In answer to that, Paul uses a fascinating play on the words *yes* and *no*. Again, I call on the Phillips translation: "Do you think I plan with my tongue in my cheek, saying 'yes' and meaning 'no' to suit my own wishes? We solemnly assure you that as certainly as God is faithful so we have never given you a message meaning 'yes' and 'no.' "

And then he comes with that powerful word: "[Jesus] is the divine 'yes.' Every promise of God finds its affirmative in him, and through him can be said the final amen, to the glory of God."

Think about it. Jesus is God's divine "yes." Think of all the profound questions to which God says "yes" in Jesus Christ. Do you love me? Am I forgiven? Am I secure in your love? Is there purpose for my life? Is there life beyond the grave?

To all these questions God has sounded an everlasting "yes" in Jesus Christ. And that "yes" can never be a "no."

Now, here is the big point. Jesus is God's "yes" to all those "no's," all those destructive don'ts that have shaped our lives.

In the next two days we will consider how the divine Yes works in our lives to enable us to overcome the destructive don'ts. For now, let's try to get the image and the experience clear.

Reflecting and Recording

Write a few sentences describing your experience of Jesus being God's divine Yes to the following questions we may ask God.

Do you love me?

_____

_____

_____

_____

Am I forgiven?

_____

_____

_____

_____

Is there purpose for my life?

_____

_____

_____

_____

Is there life beyond the grave?

_____

_____

_____

_____

During the Day

Copy this verse and place it someplace where you will see it often—
the bathroom mirror, the dashboard of your car, the refrigerator door.
JESUS IS THE DIVINE YES. EVERY PROMISE OF GOD FINDS
ITS AFFIRMATIVE IN HIM, AND THROUGH HIM CAN BE
SAID THE FINAL AMEN, TO THE GLORY OF GOD.

Claim the promise every time you think of it or read it.

| Day Six |

CONFIDENCE WITHOUT ARROGANCE

BECAUSE THE DIVINE YES HAS BEEN SPOKEN, you can be confident without
being arrogant. Isn't this our need—to be confident? To be confident
without being arrogant.

The less secure we humans are, the more we rely on superficial
props such as rank, title, degree, and recognition. The more insecure we

are, the more we seek to prove ourselves. On Day One of Week Three, I talked about my own proving game: "See here, I am worthy of your love and acceptance."

Eventually, God's love and acceptance became unquestionably real. It didn't come easily or quickly or without struggle and pain. But it came. I interiorized the acceptance and love of others.

For the first time in my life, I could stand and face the world, eyeball to eyeball; I could face the ugly and the beautiful, the stranger and the friend, the domineering and the subservient. I could stand before God and everybody and say, "Here I am, *Maxie Dunnam!*" Not aggressively, yet without apology. Not proving myself, but simply *being*.

Tom Wolfe, a contemporary writer put it this way: "The idea was to prove at every foot of the way up that pyramid that you were one of the elected and anointed ones who had the right stuff and could move higher and higher, and even that you might one day join the special few at the top, that elite . . . of the right stuff itself" (Shelby, August 16, 1981).

When we try to elbow our way to the top, to win by intimidation, to call attention to ourselves with trappings and pomp, betraying our glaring lack of both, we are still not trusting, still not willing to risk and be vulnerable. Our lives are still being shaped by destructive don'ts.

But when we know that the divine yes has been spoken, that God has said yes to us, loves us, forgives us, accepts us, we can be confident without being arrogant.

There is a fascinating and challenging word about confidence in Hebrews 13:5-6:

Keep your lives free from the love of money, and be content
with what you have; for he has said, "I will never leave you or
forsake you." So we can say with confidence,
"The Lord is my helper;
    I will not be afraid.
What can anyone do to me?"

In his classic devotional book, *My Utmost for His Highest*, Oswald Chambers has a challenging commentary on this passage from Hebrews. His theme is "God's Say-So."

My say-so is to be built on God's say-so. God says—"I will never leave thee," then I can with good courage say—"The Lord is my helper, I will not fear"—I will not be haunted by apprehension. This does not mean that I will not be tempted to fear, but I will remember God's say-so. I will be full of courage, like a child 'bucking himself up' to reach the standard his father wants. Faith in many a one falters when the apprehensions come, they forget the meaning of God's say-so, forget to take a deep breath spiritually. The only way to get the dread taken out of us is to listen to God's say-so.

What are you dreading? You are not a coward about it, you are going to face it, but there is a feeling of dread. When there is nothing and no one to help you, say—"But the Lord is my Helper, this second, in my present outlook." Are you learning to say things after listening to God, or are you saying things and trying to make God's word fit in? Get hold of the Father's say-so, and then say with good courage—"I will not fear." It does not matter what evil or wrong may be in the way, He has said—"I will never leave thee." (Chambers, p. 157)

When we accept God's say-so, the divine yes in Jesus Christ, we can be confident without being arrogant.

Reflecting and Recording

Spend some time looking at your life in terms of the tension between confidence and humility. Have you been able to be confident without being arrogant? Has the Christian call to humility hindered your development of confidence?

During the Day

God's say-so is "I will never leave you or forsake you." Claim that promise and live this day knowing that the Lord is your helper, and there is no need to be afraid.

Day Seven

ASSERTIVE WITHOUT BEING SELF-SERVING

IN ORDER TO OVERCOME THE DESTRUCTIVE DON'TS, we've got to be assertive. But assertiveness does not have to be self-serving.

I read recently of a husband who was berating his wife for her extravagant spending. "How many times do I have to tell you," he warned with a superior air, "that it's economically unsound to spend money before you get it?"

That didn't intimidate her one bit. She replied, "Oh I don't know about that. This way, if you don't get the money, at least you have something to show for it."

That woman was asserting herself, but maybe in a self-serving way. We have to find a balance between assertiveness and being self-serving. People today are groping for a new lifestyle to fit our age. People are encouraged to be assertive and to stand on their own two feet. We have many books which summon people to look out for number one, to get a piece of the action while the getting is good.

One such book was boldly entitled *The Art of Getting Your Own Sweet Way,* and the publisher's blurb promises: "Here's the scientific way for getting what you want . . . and getting other people to do what you want them to." Churches have jumped on the bandwagon and now have whole seminars on assertiveness training, psychologizing the teachings of Jesus to corroborate this particular emphasis.

> A careful reading of our Lord's teachings and attitudes reveals that Jesus indeed emphasized the rights, the worth and uniqueness of every person. His ministry broke down artificial and self-imposed barriers and broke open the stifled confines of human hearts. He recovered the lost dignity and self-esteem in souls who slouched in fear. He encouraged people to claim their God-given privileges and stature. (Shelby, August 16, 1981)

Now, give attention to this word of Jesus:

> He called the crowd with his disciples, and said to them, "If any want to become my followers, let them deny themselves

and take up their cross and follow me. For those who want to save their life will lose it, and those who lose their life for my sake, and for the sake of the gospel, will save it. For what will it profit them to gain the whole world and forfeit their life? Indeed, what can they give in return for their life?"

—Mark 8:34-37

How do we balance this call of Jesus to be servants with his emphasis on the uniqueness and worth of every person, his inspiration to people to move out of doubt and fear to triumphant faith and hope? When we find this balance, we have an assertiveness that is not self-serving. The key is accepting and respecting ourselves, and out of the strength of that identity, giving ourselves in love and service to others.

It's really a matter of *claiming our place* without denying another her place.

Having kept too close company with destructive don'ts, we tend to think we're nothing, and we don't have a place. But the divine yes has been spoken. We have a place and we can claim that place without robbing another of his or her place.

In God's kingdom, in which we are called to live now as Christians, everybody has a place. God's Yes in Jesus makes that possible.

Reflecting and Recording

When we accept Jesus Christ as God's Yes, we can be confident without being arrogant, and we can be assertive without being self-serving.

Go back to your "Reflecting and Recording" on Day One. Look at your list of don'ts. Think how these have shaped your life and how Jesus as the divine Yes may provide reshaping direction and power.

During the Day

Scrutinize your attitudes and actions today. Test yourself to see if you are being confident without being arrogant, assertive without being self-serving.

GROUP MEETING FOR WEEK FOUR

NOTE: The leader for this week should bring a chalkboard or newsprint to the group meeting. See the first suggestion under "Sharing Together" below.

Introduction

Paul advised the Philippians to "let your conversation be as it becometh the gospel" (Phil. 1:27, KJV). Most of us have yet to see the dynamic potential of the conversation which takes place in an intentional group such as this. The Elizabethan word for *life* as used in the King James Version is *conversation*, thus Paul's word to the Philippians. Life is found in communion with God and also in conversation with others.

Speaking and listening with this sort of deep meaning that communicates life is not easy.

On Day Three, we considered the destructive "don't be vulnerable." The more free we are to tell our story, the more open we are for change and healing.

So, be as open and vulnerable as you can be, knowing that each person's story is a gift and may be a healing grace for someone else.

Sharing Together

1. Ask everyone to turn to page 85 where they listed the "don'ts" that have been planted in their minds through the years. As members of the group call them out, the leader will record these on a chalkboard or newsprint. Make the list with input from each person in the group.

A. Now do a tally as to how many persons listed the same particular "don't" on their individual list.

B. Spend a few minutes discussing how all these don'ts have been destructive in our lives, or how they have served you well. As you talk, you may want to put an X by those that have been negative and a checkmark (√) by those that have been positive. Pay attention to the fact that what may have been positive to one is negative to another.

2. Move from this general discussion of destructive don'ts shaping our lives to the particular and personal. On Day Three, we considered the negative aspects of refusing to be vulnerable, and on Day Four we focused on the destructive role a refusal to trust plays in our lives. Invite three or four people to share their personal story of the power of these

don'ts working in their lives. Hopefully these will be witnesses in both areas: vulnerability and trust.

Don't rush the sharing. Take the time for persons to tell their story.

3. Spend a few minutes talking about our being taught not to be vulnerable and not to trust, and how our experience in these areas may have influenced our understanding and experience of God.

4. Invite one or two persons to share insight about themselves that came from considering the questions for "Reflection and Recording" on Day Four (page 92).

5. Invite one or two persons to witness to their experience of Jesus being God's yes in their lives.

Praying Together

1. Corporate prayer is one of the great blessings of Christian community. To affirm that is one thing; to experience it is another. To *experience* it we have to *experiment* with the possibility. Will you become a bit bolder now, and experiment with the possibilities of corporate prayer by sharing more openly and intimately?

Spend two to three minutes in silence, reflecting on your experience with the workbook this week, and the group sharing. Is there a specific need in your life—forgiveness, emotional healing for some destructive don't in your life, reconciliation with the persons who imposed destructive don'ts on you, a need to risk and be more "silly," to be confident without arrogance, or assertive without self-serving?

2. Let each person who will, share one need for forgiveness and/or healing. As this is done, other persons in the group may find it helpful to take notes on this sharing, so you can pray in a more specific way.

3. There is a sense in which, through this sharing, you have already been corporately praying. As stated earlier, there is power, however, in a community on a common journey verbalizing thoughts and feelings to God in the presence of fellow pilgrims. Experiment with this possibility now.

    A. Let the leader call each person's name, pausing briefly after each name for some person in the group to offer a brief verbal prayer focused on what that person has shared. It should be as simple as, "Lord, give Jane the confidence that she is forgiven," or "Loving God, give John the sense of your healing power in his struggle with _____." Or, "Lord, enable Ann to take the initiative to be reconciled with _____." (Leader, remember to call your own name.)

B. When all names have been called and all persons prayed for, sit in silence for two minutes; be open to the strength of love that is ours in community. *Enjoy* being linked with persons who are mutually concerned.

4. If it seems appropriate, close the prayer time with a hymn or chorus, or the leader may simply offer a brief verbal prayer.

WEEK FIVE

Dealing with Guilt and Shame

GETTING SIN IN PERSPECTIVE

IN THE "BETTER-HALF" CARTOON SERIES, Bob Barnes pictures a husband and wife in their bedroom. The wife is combing her hair and "fixing" her face across the room from the husband who is struggling to get out of bed. He sits wearily on the side of the bed, bedraggled, and moans, "I hope in my next reincarnation I come back as something easier to be than a human being."

It's not easy to be a human being. Three issues in life that make it so difficult are sin, guilt, and shame. We will never know wholeness apart from dealing with these. As blood courses through our veins, so guilt and shame flow through the veins of our emotional being.

This week we will seek to get a perspective on sin, guilt, and shame, and deal with them as a part of our construction and/or recovery process.

First, *getting sin in perspective.*

As Christians, we turn to scripture to see ourselves clearly. Paul provided a poignant picture as he wrestled with these issues of sin, guilt, and shame.

> For we know that the law is spiritual; but I am of the flesh, sold into slavery under sin. I do not understand my own actions. For I do not do what I want, but I do the very thing I hate. Now if I do what I do not want, I agree that the law is good. But in fact it is no longer I that do it, but sin that dwells within me. For I know that nothing good dwells within me, that is, in my flesh. I can will what is right, but I cannot do it. For I do not do the good I want, but the evil I do not want is what I do. Now if I do what I do not want, it is no longer I that do it, but sin that dwells within me.
>
> —Romans 7:14-20

Augustine is one of the premier theologians of all time. In his classic book, *Confessions,* he told the story of his youthful escapades of stealing pears from a neighbor's tree. He recorded that late one night a group of youngsters went out to "shake down the fruit and carry it away." They took loads of fruit from it "not to eat them ourselves," he said, "but simply to throw them to the pigs." He went on to berate himself for the depth of sin this revealed. Listen to him: "This fruit gathered, I threw away, devoured in it only iniquity. There was no other reason, but foul was the evil, and I loved it."

Now why would one harmless prank such as this loom so large in Augustine's mind? By his own admission, he had taken a mistress, fathered a child out of wedlock, and indulged in every fleshly passion. Surely, any of these was more serious than stealing pears.

Augustine saw in the "pear incident" his true nature and the nature of all humankind: "foul was the evil, and I loved it." In each of us there is sin.

Now whether we talk about this in terms of original sin, or the universality of sin, doesn't matter. The fact is that since Adam and Eve, sin has been a part of every human life. This is what Paul was struggling with in our scripture lesson as he gave expression to the anguishing conflict, the constant war raging in his soul. "I want to do good but I can't. I don't want to do evil but I find myself doing it. Oh wretched man that I am—who will deliver me from this body doomed to death?" (My paraphrase.)

Get the perspective now. There is something about our fallen nature that inclines us to commit individual acts of sin—that is "words, thoughts, and deeds" that go against God's nature and God's will for us. So there is *sin,* and there are *sins.* Sin is the universal tendency to oppose God's will, to order life on our own self-centered, self-directed terms, rather than God's terms. We may call this original sin or the carnal nature or the old man or inherited sin or moral depravity or sinful nature. It is an inherent sinful disposition that inclines persons to sinful acts. As one popular writer put it, "Lead me not into temptation; I can find the way myself."

Do you get it? We're all sinners. The dynamic of *Christians under construction,* of coming to Christian maturity, is the discipline of bringing our nature, our total self—all that we are—under the Lordship of Christ, abiding in him, that we may be shaped by his Spirit into his likeness.

Reflecting and Recording

Look back over your life, beginning in your youth. Can you identify experiences such as Augustine's "pear" incident that demonstrate some *inclination*, some *force* within, over which you sometimes seem to have no control? Describe one of those experiences here.

Reread Paul's word to the Romans. Does the experience you have recalled link your feelings with Paul?

Spend a few minutes thinking about the *fact* of sin in our life, the *universality* of sin, and how you have dealt with it.

During the Day

Stay sensitive to the struggle that may go on within you today as you make decisions and relate to others.

Day Two

A PERSPECTIVE ON GUILT

IN THE PAST FEW DECADES, there has been a great movement toward guilt-free living. This is good when we have the right perspective. The problem is that so-called modern or enlightened thinkers have actually encouraged us to disregard guilt. They have done a good job in convincing vast numbers of people that sin is acceptable, that morality is relative to individual preference, that guilt and moral accountability are outdated.

So, self-indulgence is now the norm.

> To illustrate how far our culture has moved in this regard, consider the changes that have occurred in television in the past thirty years. Three decades ago a wide array of family programs featured themes suitable for young children to enjoy with their parents with no fear of embarrassment or violation of human decency. But within the time span of one generation, the airways have become flooded with primetime programs that feature sex without benefit of marriage, provocative clothing, drug addiction, homosexuality, free use of foul language, live-in relationships, teenage suicide, seductive music videos, and a general disregard for authority." (Carter, pp. 57, 58)

This kind of thinking has become a kind of religion which we may call "secular humanism." Among its devastating fallouts is a public education without a value base that is quite willing to dispense condoms and talk about safe sex, but is not willing to talk about the moral issues in sexual expression and the deadliness of sexual promiscuity; unwilling to talk about fidelity in marriage and celibacy in singleness.

Dr. Carl Menninger, the renowned psychiatrist, in his book, *Whatever Became of Sin?* gave a powerful witness in sounding a probing challenge:

> In all of the laments and reproaches made by our seers and prophets, one misses any mention of "sin," a word which used to be a veritable watchword of prophets. It was a word once in everyone's mind, but now rarely if ever heard. Does that mean that sin no longer is involved in all our troubles—sin with an "I" in the middle? Is no one any longer guilty of anything? (Menninger, p.13)

Dr. Menninger accurately argues that a life that ignores the correcting influence of guilt is a life destined for misery.

So, guilt is a necessary emotion that has a useful function.

Now don't get ahead of me. I know, as you know, because we've all experienced it, that guilt can become so exaggerated in our lives that it is more a hindrance than a help. We can become so preoccupied with our past—and many of us do this—that our present is drained of joy and we are rendered impotent and ineffective in relationships and in our life with Christ. We will consider that tomorrow as we look at shame.

Reflecting and Recording

Psalm 51, accredited to King David of Israel, is a graphic picture of the healthy role guilt plays in our life. The setting for this prayer of David is his adulterous relationship with Bathsheba. He had manipulated the death of her husband in order to have her for himself. The prophet confronts him with his sin, and his guilt sears his soul.

Have mercy on me, O God, according to your steadfast love;
according to your abundant mercy blot out my transgressions.
Wash me thoroughly from my iniquity,
and cleanse me from my sin.
For I know my transgressions,
and my sin is ever before me.
Against you, you alone, have I sinned,
and done what is evil in your sight,
so that you are justified in your sentence
and blameless when you pass judgment.
Indeed, I was born guilty,
a sinner when my mother conceived me.
You desire truth in the inward being;
therefore teach me wisdom in my secret heart.
Purge me with hyssop, and I shall be clean;
wash me, and I shall be whiter than snow.
Let me hear joy and gladness;
let the bones that you have crushed rejoice.
Hide your face from my sins, and blot out all my iniquities.
Create in me a clean heart, O God,
and put a new and right spirit within me.
Do not cast me away from your presence,
and do not take your holy spirit from me.
Restore to me the joy of your salvation,
and sustain in me a willing spirit.
Then I will teach transgressors your ways,
and sinners will return to you.
Deliver me from bloodshed, O God,

O God of my salvation, and my tongue will sing aloud of your deliverance.

—Psalm 51:1-14

Reread the Psalm and underline what speaks especially to you.

Spend some time in prayer, with a focus on your own confession of sin and guilt.

During the Day

Copy the following prayer. Put it in a place where you will see it often; i.e., dashboard of your car, refrigerator door, in your purse or wallet. Pray the prayer as often as you see it.

Create in me a clean heart, O God, and put a new and right spirit within me. Do not cast me away from your presence, and do not take your Holy Spirit from me. Restore to me the joy of your salvation, and sustain in me a willing spirit.

Day Three

A PERSPECTIVE ON SHAME

YESTERDAY, WE LOOKED AT THE DYNAMIC OF GUILT, with the particular perspective that it can play a useful role in our life.

On Day One, we looked at sin as the universal human experience, the war that rages in our soul as we struggle with the inclination to oppose God's will, to do that which we know is destructive to our best selves, even physically and emotionally destructive.

Consider more of Paul's testimony concerning this civil war within.

For I know that nothing good dwells within me, that is, in my flesh. I can will what is right, but I cannot do it. For I do not do the good I want, but the evil I do not want is what I do. Now if

I do what I do not want, it is no longer I that do it, but sin that dwells within me. So I find it to be a law that when I want to do what is good, evil lies close at hand. For I delight in the law of God in my inmost self, but I see in my members another law at war with the law of my mind, making me captive to the law of sin that dwells in my members. Wretched man that I am! Who will rescue me from this body of death? Thanks be to God through Jesus Christ our Lord!

—Romans 7:18-25

Sin, guilt, and shame are all tied together. Today we consider shame.

Shame is closely akin to guilt. While there is something healthy about guilt, there is little that is healthy about shame.

Shame is helpful when it tells us that what we are doing is not appropriate, but only if it separates *who* we are from our behavior. But more often than not, shame is devastating and destructive.

Shame on you! The words are a curse, a spell others cast on us. It's a spell we learn to cast on ourselves. The creepy, crawling muck drips like black ink from our heads to our toes. Whether the spell is cast with a look, certain words, a tone of voice, or an old message inside our heads, it's there until we do something about it. The spell says, "What you did isn't okay, who you are isn't okay, and nothing you do will change that. *Shame on you.* (Beattie, p.102)

What happens to many of us, and especially to addicts, is that shame confuses us and becomes very destructive in our lives. We don't separate what we *do* from who we *are.* We are not only ashamed of what we have done, we are ashamed of who we are. That kind of shame is devastating and we will never be whole until we deal with it and overcome it.

Shame is the trademark of dysfunctional families. It comes with addictive families, where one or more people were addicted to alcohol, drugs, food, work, sex, religion, or gambling. It comes with families with problems and secrets. It comes with families whose parents, grandparents, or even great-grandparents had addictions, problems, or secrets. Shame adds fuel to the addictive fire. It's used to protect secrets and keep them in place. It's used to keep us in place. And often it's passed from generation to generation, like a fine piece of porcelain, until it rests on the mantel in our living room. . . .

Sometimes, we become shame based because of what others did to us. Victims of abuse are often plagued by shame, even though they weren't responsible for the inappropriate behavior. (Beattie, pp. 102-103)

So, they're all tied together. Our sin, guilt, and shame drive us to groaning anguish with Paul, "wretched man that I am! Who will rescue me from this body of death?" (Rom. 7:24).

During the rest of the week, we will look at practical ways of dealing with our guilt and shame. For now, underscore this: It is impossible to hang on to feelings of shame and guilt and still hope for healing and wholeness.

Reflecting and Recording
Record in a sentence or two some of your feelings of shame.

1._____

_____

2. _____

_____

3. _____

_____

Look at each of these. Are you responsible for them, or were they imposed by someone else, or something over which you had no control?

Perhaps things you have done were not okay; but, have you allowed what you have done to make you feel that *you* are not okay? Try to get what you have done and who you are in perspective.

During the Day
Continue praying David's prayer, which you copied yesterday.

$$\boxed{\textit{Day Four}}$$

KNOW YOUR SIN, BUT DO NOT WALLOW IN IT

ONE OF OUR PROBLEMS IS THAT WE HAVE BEEN DUPED by the pervasive philosophy of secular humanism, the philosophy of moral relativism— that we humans are the measure of all things, that there are no ultimate values or any ultimate judgment. When we feel guilty or shameful, it's not our actions or relationships that are wrong. We're just old-fashioned and we need to slough off these values and these Victorian strictures.

This is a false understanding of human nature. Its most glaring limitation is that it leaves God out of the human equation. The psalmist knew this would not work.

O Lord, you have searched me and known me.
You know when I sit down and when I rise up;
   you discern my thoughts from far away.
You search out my path and my lying down,
   and are acquainted with all my ways.
Even before a word is on my tongue,
O Lord, you know it completely.
You hem me in, behind and before,
   and lay your hand upon me;
   it is so high that I cannot attain it.

Where can I go from your spirit?
   Or where can I flee from your presence?
If I ascend to heaven, you are there;
if I make my bed in Sheol, you are there.
If I take the wings of the morning
and settle at the farthest limits of the sea,
even there your hand shall lead me,
and your right hand shall hold me fast.
I say, "Surely the darkness shall cover me,

and the light around me become night."
Even the darkness is not dark to you;
the night is as bright as the day,
for darkness is as light to you.

For it was you who formed my inward parts;
you knit me together in my mother's womb. . . .
Search me, O God, and know my heart;
test me and know my thoughts.
See if there is any wicked way in me,
and lead me in the way everlasting.
—Psalm 139:1-13, 23-24

For health and wholeness, for dealing with our guilt and shame, we must know our sin, but not wallow in it. Blaise Pascal (1623-1662) said, "We can only know God well when we know our own sin. And those who have known God without knowing their wretchedness have not glorified him, but have glorified themselves."

It's very important to know our sin. It is in knowing our sin that a healthy guilt and a healthy shame will lead us to constructive change. The psalmist also prayed, "Prove me, O Lord, and try me; test my heart and my mind" (26:2). If we do not allow the Lord to examine us in this way, we become prisoners of our sin; but we also set ourselves up for pervasive guilt and shame that will eventually mar our lives.

As indicated yesterday, it is impossible to hang on to feelings of shame and guilt and still hope for healing and wholeness. Yet to know these feelings, to seek to ascertain their source is essential. Were we treated badly by someone we love? Were we sexually, or in other physical and emotional ways abused, and the shame of that still devastates us? Have we allowed our shame to poison us against ourselves, causing us to disrespect, even punish ourselves, or to act disrespectfully toward others? Are we harboring a feeling of rottenness inside because we are unwilling to face the necessity for change?

It is important to know our sin—to know the source of guilt and shame, but that doesn't mean that we have to wallow in it. We must trust the Lord, we must accept for ourselves the gift of salvation. In the very depth of our being we must claim that promise of scripture, "If we confess our sins, he [Jesus] who is faithful and just will forgive our sins and cleanse us of all unrighteousness" (1 John 1:9). That's the beginning point of overcoming guilt and shame—know our sin, but not wallow in it.

Do you remember the story of the prodigal son? He came to himself, and when he did, he went home to his father—and he went humbly, knowing his sin. He planned his speech: "I'm no longer worthy to be called your son; make me like one of your hired servants."

You know what happened. His father saw him coming down the path while he was a long way off. He ran to him, threw his arms around him, hugged him, kissed him. The Greek verb that is used here is *continuous*, meaning he kept on kissing him and kissing him!

There was no eating the servants' food—a feast was prepared. There was no being a hired person on the farm—the best clothes were ordered and a ring to confirm the fact that he was a part of the family.

Sure, we're to know our sin and to humble ourselves in the most sincere penitence before God—but we don't stay there. We must not wallow in our sin. God is such a lover—God loves to love. Like the father in the story of the prodigal son, God will hug us and kiss us and cause us to stand tall and look him straight in the eye. God's desire is that our heart be united with his heart. Yes, we are to know our sin, but not wallow in it.

Reflecting and Recording

Spend a few minutes examining yourself. Are you guilty of wallowing in your sins? Have you confessed your sins, yet you hang on to them in your memory, with the growing questions about whether you are forgiven and loved by God?

Offer a sincere confession of sin, and accept God's forgiveness.

During the Day

On Day One I asked you to be sensitive to the struggle that may go on within you as you make decisions and relate to others. Are you more aware of that "struggle"? Test your awareness today.

Day Five

BE PATIENT WITH YOURSELF

THE LAW OF LIFE IS GROWTH. At the beginning of this workbook adventure, on Day One of Week One, I contended that *process*, not *perfection*, is what life is about. Jesus gave us a wonderful picture of growth as he talked about the nature of the kingdom of God.

> The kingdom of God is as if someone would scatter seed on the ground, and would sleep and rise night and day, and the seed would sprout and grow, he does not know how. The earth produces of itself, first the stalk, then the head, then the full grain in the head. But when the grain is ripe, at once he goes in with his sickle, because the harvest has come.
> —Mark 4:26-29

As is true with nature, so with our lives; so much is beyond our control; in fact, we control so little. And certainly, the *timing* of things is beyond our knowing or determining. So we have to be patient with ourselves, patient while we learn, patient while we grow.

This is especially relevant to dealing with guilt and shame. Paul gave us a good pattern when he wrote to the Philippians.

> Beloved, I do not consider that I have made it my own; but this one thing I do: forgetting what lies behind and straining forward to what lies ahead, I press on toward the goal for the prize of the heavenly call of God in Christ Jesus.
> —Philippians 3:13-14

The poet, Rainer Maria Rilke, expressed it beautifully: "Have patience with everything unresolved in your heart and . . . try to love *the questions themselves.*"

The desire for instant satisfaction is one of our primary spiritual problems. This is what breeds impatience—expecting everything to happen at once.

Impatience, the desire for instant satisfaction, becomes a lifestyle that blocks rich experience and possibilities for growth. If we are not willing to face and stay with another long enough to resolve conflict, we miss the joy of renewed and deeper understanding. If we do not accept the fact that spiritual growth comes in steps, and often slowly, then we will not experience the meaningful increments that come over a period of time, each building on the other; nor will we know the expansive meaning of meditation and prayer that comes only through practice.

We must be patient with ourselves. In *Touchstones, a Book of Daily Meditations for Men,* we are well taught:

> In getting to know ourselves, we don't find what we had expected. If we did, we would only be proving what we already knew. Sometimes growth comes in surprising ways. It may be in acceptance and learning to love what is unsettled or unclear within. Some of us men want to rush through our learning and push our growth too fast. Others of us want to have a strong sense of confidence in our relationships with others but always feel vulnerable. Some wonder why their fears suddenly rise without warning. Another longs to know why certain things happened to him in his youth. Our growth is not our invention. When answers come, they are gifts, and we do not control them.
>
> In part, self-acceptance is to say, "Yes, I am a person with this question, this unsettled feeling. Being alive is to be actively engaged in knowing and loving my questions even when I find no answer."

Certainly what is said here about men is true also of women.

Reflecting and Recording

Finish the following sentences.

I am impatient with myself when . . .

I have trouble accepting and forgiving when . . .

What do these statements about impatience say about your acceptance of yourself as a normal human being?

What do these statements say about your feelings of guilt and shame?

During the Day

Memorize this prayer:

"Loving Christ, grant me the peace that comes with loving the unfinished part of me."

Pray it through the day.

Day Six

Be Patient with Others

A POPULAR MOTTO THAT HAS BEEN PRINTED on bumper stickers and posters begs, "Be patient with me. God isn't finished with me yet."

A prayer that has also made it on posters and other forms for public consumption captures the same thought: "I am not what I ought to be, and I'm not what I'm going to be, but praise God, I am not what I used to be."

If we would make these affirmations for ourselves, we must allow others to make them for themselves. Not only must we be patient with ourselves, we must be patient with others.

A counselor sat through the complaints a woman kept making against her husband. Finally he said, "Your marriage would be a happier one if you were a better wife."

"And how could I be that?" asked the woman.

The counselor responded, "By giving up your efforts to make him a better husband."

The counselor was right, and it works the other way, also. A man becomes a better husband when he ceases trying to make his mate a better wife.

Aren't we all guilty—not just in marriage, but in all relationships? We think things would be different if we could just change the other person.

One of the biggest issues in relationships is patience. Others are a source of our guilt and shame—and we have to know that. But we have to be patient with them—because they know shame and guilt also. They have not yet arrived either. They are growing. So we have to be patient with others.

We have to remember that what is true of ourselves is also true of others—individuals develop at their own pace. It will help us also to reflect on what God has done in our life, as well as in the lives of others.

When we do this, we can be patient, knowing that as some positive and redemptive change has taken place, other changes will come in time.

We can develop and express our patience with others in two ways. One, by *refocusing our expectations.* Unfilled expectations are the source of much of the hurt we carry around in our hearts. People have not and will not always meet our needs.

While God intends for us to fulfill certain needs of each other, God also knows we fail. If we can refocus our point of dependence from others to God, then in God's sovereignty and timing our needs will be met.

Two, we can *release others.* This is a way of refocusing our expectations. In terms of shame and guilt this is especially true of our parents and other loved ones who may have caused much of the pain in our lives. We can release them from our bitter judgment, and suppressed condemnation by forgiving them. Jesus made it very clear:

> For if you forgive others their trespasses, your heavenly Father will also forgive you; but if you do not forgive others, neither will your Father forgive your trespasses.
>
> —Matthew 6:14-15

As we must be patient and forgiving with ourselves, we must be patient and forgiving with others. Time heals our wounds and teaches us lessons we can't learn in a day. If we will be patient and forgiving, we will discover that answers come and relationships are often healed simply by waiting.

By refocusing our expectations and releasing others by forgiveness, we can free ourselves and others from the unfair demand to change quickly. This kind of patience also enables us to deal with troubling work situations, our anger about our addictions, and many other side issues of guilt and shame.

Reflecting and Recording

Fill in the blanks with the names of three persons you need to be patient with.

_____

_____

_____

Now look at these names. Does being patient with them involve refocusing expectations and releasing them by forgiveness? Make notes beside each name, indicating specific responses and action you need to take to make your patience real.

During the Day

As you relate to the special people in your life today, examine yourself with these questions:

(1) Am I being inconsiderate?

(2) Am I being selfish?

(3) Am I being dishonest?

Day Seven

BE PATIENT WITH GOD

ONE OF MY FAVORITE AFFIRMATIONS OF SCRIPTURE is Philippians 1:6: "I am confident of this, that the one who began a good work among you will bring it to completion by the day of Jesus Christ."

Although it may sound like a strange idea, not only must we be patient with ourselves, and patient with others, we must be patient with God.

God has a timetable—and we can't control that. And there are other factors involved as well. One huge one is the freedom of people to respond to God. How long have you been praying for a loved one to come to Jesus Christ? That has not yet happened and you grow weary.

How many times have you asked God to remove that thorn from your flesh? But the thorn is still there. We must be patient. God has reasons we don't know about.

How many times have you prayed for the sobriety of a husband or a wife or a child? And yet they still go their way, victimized by that awful power that has them in its clutches.

You've got to be patient with God. The only way that patience can be kept alive and grow is to continue to believe that God is faithful. Paul put it this way: "I am confident of this, that the one who began a good work among you will bring it to completion by the day of Jesus Christ." God has promised. God is faithful. And God will complete that work in you and in others. But you'll have to be patient: patient with yourself, patient with others, and patient with God.

We do identify with Paul in his struggle expressed in Romans 7 (verses 19, 24) don't we? "For I do not do the good I want, but the evil I do not want is what I do. . . . Wretched man that I am! Who will rescue me from this body of death?" Who will rescue me from this body of guilt and shame?

But do we go on with Paul and claim with confidence what he claims in verse 25: "Thanks be to God through Jesus Christ our Lord!" And verse 1 of chapter 8: "There is therefore now no condemnation for those who are in Christ Jesus." We don't have to be victims of guilt and shame.

Benjamin West (1738-1820), the renowned artist, tells about how he became a painter. One day his mother went out, leaving him in charge of his little sister Sally. He discovered some bottles of colored ink and began to paint Sally's portrait. He really made a mess of things. Ink blots were all over. On her return the mother saw the mess. But grace prevailed. She said nothing, picked up one piece of paper, and saw the drawing. "It's Sally," she said immediately and excited and then gave Benjamin a kiss. Later, this great painter, said, "My mother's kiss made me a painter."

God's kiss of grace makes us Christian—but like the father in the story of the prodigal son, God keeps on kissing us, and it is that *ongoing kiss of grace* that will enable us to use guilt and shame for our good and God's glory.

Reflecting and Recording

Spend some time considering your *impatience* with God. Be honest in facing these feelings that you may not have identified in this fashion.

Sometimes our praying is more expressive and powerful when we discipline ourselves to write the prayer. Writing forces us to be reflective, precise, and honest. I call this "praying at the point of a pencil."

Write on the next page your prayer expressing yourself to God about your failure/desire/commitment in being patient with yourself, patient with others, and patient with God.

During the Day

If there is someone with whom you have not been patient and you want to ask forgiveness, call, write, or see that person today.

Continue to pray that prayer you memorized on Day Five of this week.

"Loving Christ, grant me the peace that comes with loving the unfinished part of me."

GROUP MEETING FOR WEEK FIVE

Introduction

John Wesley called on Christians to use all the "means of grace" available for their Christian walk, their growth in Christlikeness. Along with the ones that we normally think of—prayer, scripture, study, worship, holy communion—Wesley named Christian conferencing. By it, he meant intentional Christian conversation, talking about spiritual matters, and sharing our Christian walk.

Sharing Together

1. You have finished five weeks of this workbook journey. Spend a few minutes talking about the experience in general terms. What is giving you difficulty? What is providing the most meaning?

2. Invite one person to share the experience recorded on Day One as a "pear" incident that demonstrates some *inclination*, some *force* within, over which he or she sometimes seems to have no control.

3. Spend five to eight minutes talking about the *fact* of sin in our life. Do you argue that sin is universal?

4. Spend five to eight minutes talking about the connection between guilt and shame.

5. Invite two or three persons to share their own experience of shame that has been a negative, even destructive, force in their lives.

122 THE WORKBOOK ON CHRISTIANS UNDER CONSTRUCTION AND IN RECOVERY

6. Looking at these experiences of shame, reflect and talk about the difficulty of separating what we *do* from who we *are*—and how this confusion is detrimental to our healing and wholeness.

7. Spend a brief three to four minutes clarifying this statement: "A healthy guilt and a healthy shame will lead us to constructive change."

8. Invite the group to spend a bit of time reviewing their workbook notes for this week to identify issues or questions raised that they would like to talk about. Spend the balance of your time (saving time for prayer) responding to these questions and issues.

Praying Together

Spontaneous conversational prayer—persons offering brief sentences—is a powerful dynamic in our group life. One person may offer a sentence or two now, and then again after two or three others have prayed. One person's prayer may suggest another. Don't try to say everything in your one prayer. Pray pointedly, knowing you can pray again during this time of prayer. This way you can be spontaneous and not strain to make sure you have "covered all the bases."

Share prayer requests before you begin your actual praying.

1. Are there persons in the group who have expressed shame and/or guilt who need to be prayed for specifically?

2. Is there someone needing help in forgiving someone else?

3. Does a person need to forgive himself or herself and be willing to share it with the group?

4. Does any person wish specific prayers for being more patient with self, others, or God? Respond to these specific needs with conversational prayer.

WEEK SIX

Getting Ourselves Out of Hock

YOU SHOW ME THE PATH OF LIFE

I STRUGGLE BETWEEN LIKE AND DISLIKE, appreciation and confusion, with Gary Larson's "The Far Side" cartoons. I keep on reading them, and I'm not quite sure why. Maybe it's because he gives me something now and then to flavor a sermon, or to add spice to a conversation. Then there are those times when his message is profound. Such is the case with the one which depicted a bug resting on a leaf which gently sways over a lovely pond. The bug is on his back in the crook of the leaf, his ankles are crossed, and two of his six arms are crossed behind his head. "Ahhhhh, this is the life!" he is saying. Unknown to him, the eyes of a huge frog surface from the pond directly beneath his leaf. Frogs love bugs.

Some of us are oblivious to the enemies that lie in wait to gobble us up. But most of us are aware of them—aware to the point of pain and even dysfunction. That's the reason for this workbook: to make us aware, if we're not already, of the crippling, even killing forces that control our lives, to give us hope and resources for fighting battles with our enemies, and to give us direction to move in paths of recovery and wholeness.

This week, our theme is *getting ourselves out of hock.*

Do you understand that image? The image is most real in a pawn shop.

It may surprise some readers to know that I visit pawn shops now and then. In fact, that may strike you as weird. I like auctions and estate sales. I don't like flea markets too much, but I hardly ever go to London without going to the Portabella Flea Market or the one at Angels Crossing.

I've never hocked anything—but I've bought a few things at pawn shops—for instance, tools. In the pawn shop system, you hock something—a ring or a watch—for an amount of money. You pay interest on that money, but the pawn shop owner holds your item for three months, or as long as you pay interest on it, or pay what you borrowed and get your item out of hock.

My contention is that we put ourselves into hock, and sometimes events or circumstances put us there.

Persons recovering from addiction know this with certainty; it is true to some degree with all of us.

Serenity: A Companion for Twelve Step Recovery is an edition of the New Testament, Psalms, and Proverbs. Though a presentation of scripture supporting persons in programs using the Twelve Steps of Alcoholics Anonymous, it is a helpful devotional resource for any of us.

The *Serenity Bible* lists scripture passages to read for meditation with each of the twelve steps. Also, the material in the scripture itself that has to do with a particular step is shaded and the step to which it is related is designated in the margin.

I found this very helpful because steps five and six of AA have to do with getting our lives out of hock. The scripture designated as support for step six is Psalm 16:7-11.

Here are steps five and six.

> (5) Admitted to God, to ourselves, and to another human being the exact nature of our wrongs.

> (6) Were entirely ready to have God remove all these defects of character.

Here is the psalm.

> I bless the Lord, who gives me counsel;
> My heart also instructs me in the night seasons.
> I have set the Lord always before me;
> Because He is at my right hand I shall not be moved.
> Therefore my heart is glad, and my glory rejoices;
> My flesh also will rest in hope.
> For You will not leave my soul in Sheol,
> Nor will You allow Your Holy One to see corruption.
> You will show me the path of life;
> In Your presence is fullness of joy;
> At Your right hand are pleasures forevermore.
> —Psalm 16:7-11, NKJV

Concentrate on verse 11. "You will show me the path of life; In Your presence is fullness of joy; At Your right hand are pleasures forevermore."

Reflecting and Recording

Spend some time thinking about the image, "my life in hock." In what ways is your life in hock? What forces are holding you captive? Have you exchanged something valuable in your life for something else (i.e., fidelity to your spouse for the satisfaction of sexual passion with another)? Is there some life value that you need to "redeem" (get out of hock)?

Reread the passage above from Psalm 16.

During the Day

You will show me the path of life;
In Your presence is fullness of joy;
At Your right hand are pleasures forevermore.

Copy this verse and take this with you in your pocket or purse today. Take it out now and then, reading it and rereading it until you memorize it.

Day Two

FEAR AND ANXIETY

THE MOST COMMON FORCE THAT KEEPS OUR LIFE IN HOCK is fear and anxiety. There is a *healthy* fear that protects us in time of real danger. A proper sense of fear makes us good defensive drivers, makes us wise in how we walk city streets at night, and protects us from irresponsible daredevil antics. It is a fear that is normal and necessary for life.

The unhealthy kind of fear is a neurotic fear that has us in hock, a fear that causes us to worry and brings us to the point of crippling anxiety.

An analysis of the records of a well-known medical clinic reveals that thirty-five percent of all illnesses treated in the clinic started with fear and anxiety. A life insurance company reports that four out of five nervous breakdowns began not in actual events, but with worry.

Heart failure and diseases resulting from stress and hypertension rapidly are becoming the major killers among all ailments. Much of this is rooted in fear and anxiety.

These facts are even more startling when we realize that a baby is born with only two normal fears: the fear of loud noises and the fear of falling. All other anxieties are acquired, and most of us have acquired a goodly number.

Ask yourself, what are the fears that have my life in hock? Fear of failure? Fear of not being able to stay sober? Fear about the security of my present employment? Fear about my children's future? Fear of old age? Fear of death? Fear of inadequacy? And for addicts, this fear of inadequacy is coupled with humiliation and shame.

We could go on. Fear does have many of our lives in hock.

Reflecting and Recording

On the lines below, list your most dominant fears. Go beyond the surface. Search deeply.

_____

_____

_____

_____

Now look at each of these fears. What is the source of these fears? Has something happened to make you fearful? Is some person responsible? The circumstances of your life?

Make notes beside each listed fear, answering these questions.

I join many psychologists and counselors in contending that the only known cure for fear is faith! For the Christian, that faith is in Christ who said, "In the world you face persecution. But take courage; I have conquered the world!" (John 16:33).

We are loved by Christ. Accepting that love and seeking to express it, we overcome fear. The disciple John put it this way:

> Love has been perfected among us in this: that we may have boldness on the day of judgment, because as he is, so are we in this world. There is no fear in love, but perfect love casts out fear; for fear has to do with punishment, and whoever fears has not reached perfection in love. We love because he first loved us.
>
> —1 John 4:17-19

Ponder this truth for two or three minutes in relation to your fears recorded above: *Because Christ loves me, I can overcome fear with love.*

During the Day

If you have not memorized it, continue to read Psalm 16:11, which you copied yesterday. Repeat it enough to make it a part of your consciousness. Throughout the day, stay aware that "love casts out fear." In the confidence of God's love, there is joy, not fear.

Day Three

COMPULSION TO RESCUE

DO YOU FEEL DRIVEN? Are there times when you seem to be out of control—you are carried along by some inside force you have not yet identified? Do you find yourself acting without deciding to act—acting sometimes in ways you abhor? Your life may be in hock to compulsion.

I know, as many readers will quickly begin to think, that the compulsive personality is most apt to become an addict. We usually think of that in terms of blatant addiction—alcohol and other drugs. But too many of us have a knack for overlooking our own tendencies toward compulsions of various types. But when we think of compulsions or compulsiveness more broadly than in the stereotypical addict, we see its relevance to most of us.

Let me mention briefly three directions for compulsiveness that may have your life in hock.

Kenneth A. Schmidt calls these the three faces of sin. He sees this in the temptation of Jesus by Satan in the wilderness. Look at the story.

> Jesus, full of the Holy Spirit, returned from the Jordan and was led by the Spirit in the wilderness, where for forty days he was tempted by the devil. He ate nothing at all during those days, and when they were over, he was famished. The devil said to him, "If you are the son of God, command this stone to become a loaf of bread. Jesus answered him, "It is written, 'One does not live by bread alone.'"
>
> —Luke 4:1-4

The temptation for Jesus was to use his power to escape his pain by turning stones into bread. Schmidt identifies this as the temptation to rescue.

> It's usually appropriate for us to stop our pain, for it indicates something is amiss and needs attention. But the action we take must fit the pain we're experiencing. If the pain of hunger is only telling us the body needs food, eating bread is an appropriate response. The Spirit led Jesus to His pain, however, to give Him opportunity to obey. So the question Jesus faced in this temptation was "Do I rescue Myself from My immediate need rather than remaining true to My relationship with My Father?"
>
> Jesus responded, "Man does not live by bread alone." To rescue Himself from pain at the cost of His relationship with God would have been to set His goals above His Father's (Schmidt, p. 81).

Schmidt calls this—the temptation to rescue—one of the three faces of sin. It is that, a compulsiveness to which some of our lives are in hock.

It is one of the ways *we play God*. We play God by being good. We talked about this in Week Two under the rubric "When being good is bad for you."

> The motto of Rescuers is "I should and I can." They're willing to carry other's burdens, even when it's damaging to

both of them. They have effectively hidden their own need and are often described as "wonderful" because they seem so caring.

At first glance, Rescuers appear to be very Christian, but it's a deception. Their goodness is not a natural outflowing of love but a facade covering a lack of feeling and love. They can't face their emptiness, so they try to be recognized and loved for doing good." (Schmidt, p. 98)

The compulsion to rescue. Do you have that kind of compulsion; or, do you find yourself in hock to someone who is always rescuing you?

Reflecting and Recording

It is not easy to recognize this compulsion to rescue. It is very difficult to label and deal with it because it is so acceptable. Schmidt suggests a clue we might use to explore this compulsion: a lack of genuine emotional response. Though we do the right things, we don't feel life and joy.

Use that clue to examine your own compulsion to rescue.

Continue your self-examination by focusing on this question: Am I so intent on rescuing myself from immediate pain and need that I miss cultivating lasting values and relationships that will have continuing meaning?

During the Day

Stay aware of and resist your compulsion to rescue.

Day Four

COMPULSION TO CONTROL

JESUS' TEMPTATION IN THE WILDERNESS CONTINUES:

> Then the devil led him up and showed him in an instant all the kingdoms of the world. And the devil said to him, "To you I will give their glory and all this authority; for it has been given over to me, and I give it to anyone I please. If you, then, will worship me, it will all be yours." Jesus answered him, "It is written,
>   'Worship the Lord your God,
>   and serve only him.' "
>
> —Luke 4:5-8

Here is the second face of sin: the *temptation to control.* For Jesus this would have been another way to avoid pain. Rather than being submissive to and worshipping God, he could take control and make things different. This is a "face of sin," but let's deal with it as a compulsion that may have our lives in hock.

Controllers seek to get what they want by playing God.

> We hide our pain, weakness and vulnerability and present a facade of strength, self-righteousness and intimidation. We try to take away the freedom of others by creating fear or guilt within them. Controllers may be openly coercive and angry or may disguise themselves well. They may smile and say, 'This is for your own good,' while their selfish motives are hidden. They may even disguise their attacks as teasing and tell you to laugh it off, for they were "only joking." Regardless, they seem to have a knack for seeing other people's faults (and ignoring their own). (Schmidt, p.95)

I first came into touch with this compulsion in my own life twenty-five years ago. I was a participant in a pastor's growth group which was led by Everett L. Shostrom, a psychologist in Santa Ana, California. Ev became a friend. In that group, he started reading us material that he was preparing for a book which was published as *Man, the Manipulator.*

Later, I joined Ev and a clergy friend, Gary Herbertson, in writing a book entitled *The Manipulator and the Church*. That was an awful title, and the book didn't attract much attention. Yet, it dealt with some of the crucial issues of life—among them this destructive compulsion to control.

I discovered in my own life the need to control. My compulsion grew out of my feelings of inadequacy, as well as my drive to perfection. We don't normally think of these together, but they are closely related. If we feel inadequate, we overcompensate by efforts at perfect performance to prove our sufficiency and worth.

The root problem is that we don't trust our ability to live through the confusion and pain of life. Add to this the fact of our distrust of others to help us through the confusion and pain and you have a recipe for destructive control. We not only are neurotically self-controlling, we hover over others to protect them. We appoint ourselves to monitor the behavior and activity of others.

One of the primary dynamics of growth and wholeness is learning to let go.

Reflecting and Recording

Are there persons whom you feel seek to control your life? Name them.

If you do not feel the controlling effort of someone over you, can you identify some persons who you think compulsively seek to control? Name them.

Look at the persons you named. Study their attitude and behavior, their way of relating to life and to others. Make some notes about what they are like.

It is very easy for us to be aware of other persons' controlling behavior, but unaware of our own. Look now at your notes concerning others' compulsion to control. Do any of these characteristics "fit" you? Don't leave this quickly. Spend time thinking about it.

During the Day
Stay aware of and resist your temptation to control.

Day Five

COMPULSION TO BE A VICTIM

NOT ONLY DID JESUS CONFRONT THE TEMPTATIONS to *rescue* and *control*, he confronted the temptation *to be a victim*.

> Then the devil took him to Jerusalem, and placed him on the pinnacle of the temple, saying to him, "If you are the Son of God, throw yourself down from here, for it is written 'He will command his angels concerning you, to protect you,' and 'on their hands they will bear you up, so that you will not dash your foot against a stone.' "
> Jesus answered him, "It is said, 'Do not put the Lord your God to the test.' "
>
> —Luke 4:9-12

Had Jesus given in to this temptation he would have been refusing to take responsibility. By throwing himself off the precipice of the temple, he would have made himself a *victim* and forced God to save him.

Playing victim is also a way of manipulation.

> Victims avoid their pain by manipulating someone into taking care of them. They either believe they're incapable of handling the problems of life or that they shouldn't have to. 'I can't' and 'I'm not responsible' are their mottos.

Victims give others authority over them and then abdicate responsibility because of weakness. 'You're right, I should do that, but I can't' is a frequent response. They believe they can't take actions to change or improve life, so they don't try. (Schmidt, p. 102)

The compulsion to be a victim is our way of evading responsibility for choices. It's not easy to be a *choosing* person, but everyday we have choices to make. Often the options we have may be undesirable, even painful. So for some, refusing to accept responsibility for choice is the easy path. We can be victims by not deciding.

One area where the victim syndrome works is our feelings. We want someone to blame for the way we feel. When we are frustrated, angry, impotent, filled with self-pity, we want someone else to be responsible.

Recently I was talking to a man who had gone through a divorce. He had been living alone for six months. "I'm making a healthy discovery," he said, "I'm still having all those feelings that I used to blame on my wife. I can't do that now, so I'm having to take responsibility."

The playwright, Arthur Miller, said, "The perfection of innocence, indeed, is madness." The compulsion to be a victim is an expression of this madness. We don't want to do anything to hurt anybody; or more accurately, we don't want to be *blamed* for hurting anyone. "I didn't mean any harm; don't blame me" is a recurring expression of the victim.

The truth is there can be no perfection of innocence because we can't live in relationship without someone getting hurt. There is no spiritual growth without decision and taking action; and then, accepting responsibility for the outcome.

The compulsion to be a victim is fed by internal feelings of inadequacy and distrust of self. Others always taking care of them (and there are usually a lot of rescuers around to do this) only confirms their false self. When they successfully manipulate others by being victims, they rob themselves of self-esteem.

Reflecting and Recording

Kenneth A. Schmidt, whom we have been quoting about the three faces of sin, brings these faces to a focus in the family.

We must also discover and confess the faces of sin we wear with our families:

If we want to blame them because of hurts or neglect, we must confess our desire to be Controllers.

If we want to maintain our good image in their eyes more than we want to be God's children, we must confess our desire to be Rescuers.

If we desire their rescuing and support more than God's, we must confess playing the Victim role.

If we don't allow the Spirit to put these aspects of our old selves to death, they will continue to haunt us. (Schmidt, p. 152)

If you are not living in a "traditional" family, we can apply this to the circle of folks we live most intimately with, and care most about. Spend some time using Schmidt's word as a guide to examination to explore your compulsion to be either a controller, a rescuer, or a victim.

On the next two days we will look at specific action to get our life out of hock to whatever force binds us or undermines our wholeness. For now, reflect on the role honesty and confession play in our release from any destructive compulsion. We don't know how the Spirit works, but we know that the work is that of *restoration* and transformation. If we honestly pray and reveal our needs, the Spirit will work within us. Close your time of reflection by staying your mind on this promise of scripture.

Likewise the Spirit helps us in our weakness; for we do not know how to pray as we ought, but that very Spirit intercedes with sighs too deep for words. And God, who searches the heart, knows what is the mind of the Spirit, because the Spirit intercedes for the saints according to the will of God.

—Romans 8:26-27

During the Day

Stay aware of and resist your temptation to be a victim.

Day Six

TAKE THE RESPONSIBILITY THAT BELONGS TO YOU

AN ENTIRE BOOK COULD BE WRITTEN ON our focus for this week: *getting our lives out of hock.* Loneliness, anger, depression, perfectionism, resentment (and the list could go on), are some of the forces that hold us in bondage. Rather than continue exploration of these, let's look at actions we may take or attitudes we must cultivate to get our lives out of hock.

We introduced one action in closing the session yesterday: *confession.* I put it this way: *identify, bring to the surface those forces you feel are controlling your life, and confess that in your own strength you cannot prevail against them.*

Does this sound like Step One in AA? "We admitted that we were powerless over alcohol—that our lives had become unmanageable." It's an action all of us need to take to get our lives out of hock to whatever negative forces may be controlling us.

In Psalm 16, verse 4, there is this word: "Those who choose another god multiply their sorrows." Interestingly, in the *Serenity Bible,* which I mentioned on Day One of this week, this verse is shaded and marked Step One, meaning that it is scriptural support for Step One of AA.

You see, there are forces that control our lives and these forces are presently the gods (note the word *gods* is not capitalized) of our lives. They control us. They have us in hock. We must identify them, bring them to the surface as forces that are controlling our life, and confess that in our own strength we cannot prevail against them. And so we turn to Christ and invite him to be our companion in the struggle, giving us the strength we do not have within ourselves.

Now a second action: *take whatever responsibility belongs to you.*

Again I call on a "Peanuts" cartoon. In the first frame, Lucy is saying, "I want to talk to you, Charlie Brown."

In the next frame, she continues, "As your sister's consulting psychiatrist, I must put the blame for her fears on you!"

In the third frame, Charlie Brown literally shakes and almost screams, "On *me*?" And Lucy responds matter-of-factly, "Each generation must be able to blame the previous generation for its problems"—and then she concludes in the last frame, much to Charlie

Brown's puzzlement, "It doesn't solve anything, but it makes us all feel better."

Well, it may make us feel better to fix blame elsewhere, but the feeling is short-lived. To get our life out of hock, we must take whatever responsibility belongs to us.

Reflecting and Recording

Listed below are four categories of relationships. Examine your relationships in each of these areas, honestly exploring the possibility that you have not taken responsibility that belongs to you. Make notes about each area in terms of your failure and what you are going to do about it.

In my relationship to my spouse

In my relationship to my children

In my relationship to my friends

In relationship to colleagues at work

During the Day

If you do not know "The Serenity Prayer" copy it and carry it with you for the next few days, praying it as often as it comes to your attention, until you have memorized it.

God, grant me the serenity to accept the things I cannot change, the courage to change the things I can, and the wisdom to know the difference.

CEASE LIVING LIFE AS SOMETHING YOU OWE

THE THIRD SUGGESTION FOR GETTING OUR LIVES out of hock is an attitude and an action, a stance which will give us freedom—a freedom from fear and compulsion, as well as other things that hold us in emotional hock. I put it this way: *Cease living life as something you owe.*

I like the story about the man who was standing in line at a serving table and got to the chicken. "Two pieces," he said to the lady who was serving. She put one piece on the plate.

The man said, "Two pieces." The lady replied, "One piece." The man continued, "Evidently, you don't know who I am. I'm the governor of this state." The lady responded, "Evidently, you don't know who I am. I'm the lady in charge of the chicken."

I hope you don't hear this as conflicting with what I've just said about taking responsibility. We are to take responsibility, but too many of us have been neurotic about responsibility and duty. We feel guilty when anything around us goes wrong. Also, we get into a payback or a repay syndrome. "They invited us—we must invite them." "They sent us a Christmas card, we must put them on our mailing list."

Deeper and more devastating than those kinds of superficial responses to others is to think we have to repay everybody for what they have done for us. Recovering folks think they have to pay back for all the suffering and shame they have caused, all the time that they have stolen from those they love. We will always be in hock with our life if we don't overcome this neurosis. We don't need to live life as something we owe.

Psalm 16:5 says, "The Lord is my chosen portion and my cup; you hold my lot." We owe our lives only to God—not to anyone else.

Finally, to get our lives out of hock, we must keep on trusting God. This attitude of trusting God must pervade all our decisions and actions.

> Protect me, O God, for in you I take refuge. . . . You show me the path of life. In your presence there is fullness of joy; at your right hand are pleasures forevermore.
>
> —Psalm 16:1, 11

Here it is in a story. Cecil B. De Mille told about watching a water beetle that crawled up on the gunwale of his canoe, stuck the talons on his legs into the woodwork, and died. A little while later he looked at the beetle. His back was cracking open. Crawling out of the back of that dead beetle, a new form—a moist head and then wings. It was a most beautiful dragonfly, scintillating all the colors of the rainbow. Said De Mille, "If God does that for a water beetle, don't you believe He will do it for me?"

Well, God will—if we allow it. Through God's power we can get our lives out of hock.

Reflecting and Recording

Make a list of the people to whom you feel you owe something other than money.

Look at each of these names and make notes about why you feel you owe them. For instance, I would name David McKeithen, my pastor when I answered the call to preach.

Now look at each name. What is it that you really owe them? I owe David gratitude. I may owe someone else forgiveness. Make your notes beside each name.

Many of these feelings of owing people something may be very healthy. Examine yourself in light of the exercise to determine if, in an unhealthy way, you are living your life as something you owe.

Move now to think about *trusting God.* Is there any sense in which your life is in hock because you are refusing to trust God? Make notes of your reflections here.

During the Day
Continue to pray "The Serenity Prayer."

GROUP MEETING FOR WEEK SIX

Introduction

You are drawing to the close of this adventure. This meeting and the next are the last planned group meetings. At this one, your group may want to discuss the future. Would they like to stay together for a longer time? Are there books, tapes, and so forth they would like to use corporately? If you're part of the same church, is there a way they might share the experience with others in the church?

Some of the primary qualities of life essential for recovery and construction as Christians are summarized in the Greek word *hupomone*—a prominent though often neglected word in the New Testament. It is translated as *endurance, patience, steadfastness.* Recovery and construction—ongoing conversion—of life takes place not by clinging to our *mountaintop* spiritual experiences, though these are to be savored, but by living faithfully day to day, by discipline and intentional desire. Change takes place as we seek to be present to our fellow pilgrim, Jesus, and in companionship with others who are willing to share our journey. So as we reflected last week, be patient with yourself, patient with others, and patient with God.

Sharing Together

1. Begin your time together by the leader offering an opening prayer or calling on someone else (consulted ahead of time) to do so. Then sing a chorus or a couple of verses of a hymn everyone knows.

2. Ask each person to share the most meaningful insight or experience gained from this week.

3. Invite two or three persons to share the fears that at times have controlled them.

4. Invite one person to share his or her compulsion to rescue, one person to share his or her compulsion to control, and one person to share his or her compulsion to be a victim.

When the three persons have shared, spend eight to ten minutes as a group talking about these compulsions as ways we play God, and as "faces of sin." Read the quote from Schmidt about the "faces of sin" in the family on page 135 to begin this discussion.

5. If it has not come out in discussion already, discuss the suggestion that our need to control may grow out of our feelings of inadequacy and/or our drive for perfection.

As is always needful, this discussion needs to be more than an intellectual exercise; it should reflect shared personal experience.

6. The theme for this week is "Getting Ourselves Out of Hock." We focused on three compulsions that hold us in hock: to rescue, to control, and to be a victim. There are forces that hold us in bondage; i.e., loneliness, anger, depression. Invite as many persons as will to share their own experience of feeling in bondage to some of these other forces.

Praying Together

On Days Six and Seven this week, we considered two actions we might take to get our lives out of hock: (1) Take responsibility that belongs to you, and (2) cease living your life as something you owe.

As you begin your prayer time,

(1) Invite persons to share specific needs for guidance and strength at either of these points.

(2) Invite persons to share their own needs or those of friends or family members in the areas of rescuing, controlling, or being victims.

(3) Invite persons to share other needs that have been identified in the week's reflection or in the group sharing.

Now enter into a time of verbal prayer. Make sure that every need mentioned is specifically prayed for.

Close your time with the group praying aloud the Serenity Prayer on page 137.

Pay Attention to Yourself

GIVE YOURSELF TIME

YOU MUST PAY ATTENTION TO YOURSELF. Unless the wholeness journey begins here, it doesn't begin.

Leo Buscaglia tells a story that could have happened to a lot of us. He says he does a lot of work while traveling on airplanes. I can identify with that. He had settled down in a seat, and the seat between him and the passenger on the aisle was free so he thought that he would get a lot done. But the person who occupied that seat was a middle-aged-lady who wore lots of jewelry and was beautifully attired. She watched Buscaglia as he spread out his things, and he could tell she really wanted to talk. He thought to himself, "Oh my God! I love her but I have exams to grade and papers to read!"

She said, "I bet I can guess what *you* are!"

I said, "What am I?"

She said, "I'll bet you're a lawyer."

I said no, I wasn't a lawyer.

She said, "Then you're a teacher."

I said, "Yes, that's what I am. I'm a teacher."

So she said, "Oh how nice," and Buscaglia went back to his work. But she started to talk, and all of a sudden he realized what he was doing. He recognized the fact that he was always talking about people and their needs and how we should listen. An inner voice spoke to him, "You're always talking about people first. If you really mean it, this lady *needs* you. She obviously wants to talk—so talk to her awhile, then maybe you can explain your need to get to work."

As he turned his attention to her, she told him all kinds of things. She told him about her four children and that she had just come from the Bahamas and that she'd had a terrible time. She said that she'd been alone there and was trying to get her life together. Then she shed the news: "Two months ago my husband left me."

"Oh, I'm sorry," Buscaglia said. Then she started again and she told him the story of her life and her marriage.

"Imagine. I gave *him*," she said, "the best"—[really!]—the best years of my life! I gave him the best years of my life. I gave him beautiful children! I gave him a magnificent house, and I always kept it clean; there was no dust anywhere!"

The woman continued, "My children were always on time to school. I was a magnificent cook, always entertained *his* friends. I was always ready to go everyplace *he* wanted to."

She continued talking and Buscaglia began to feel sorry for her. In the process of doing the things she thought were essential, this woman had lost herself. "She had not given her husband what was essential about *her* . . . the magic, the wonder . . . the undiscovered self. She'd given him good food—he could have gone to a restaurant. She cleaned his sheets—he could have gone to a laundramat!"

Then Buscaglia asked her, "What did you do for *you*?"

She responded, "What do you mean—what do you mean for *me*?"

"I mean what did you do for *yourself*?"

"There wasn't any *time* to do anything for myself!"

As that settled in Buscaglia's mind he asked, "What would you *like* to have done?"

"Oh, I've always had a dream of throwing pots" (Buscaglia, pp. 67–69).

What a sad story. But many of us could tell a similar one. The danger threatens all of us. We might end up like that woman having lived life but not having really lived. If we are in need of recovery, if we are going to grow, we've got to pay attention to ourselves. The foundation for paying attention to ourselves is love. Do you remember Jesus' encounter with the Pharisees?

> When the Pharisees heard that he had silenced the Sadducees, they gathered together, and one of them, a lawyer, asked him a question to test him. "Teacher, which commandment in the law is the greatest?" He said to him, " 'You shall love the Lord your God with all your heart, and with all your soul, and with all your mind.' This is the greatest and first commandment. And a second is like it: 'You shall love your neighbor as yourself.' On these two commandments hang all the law and the prophets."
> —Matthew 22:34-40

As yourself is not an unimportant addition to Jesus' call for us to love others. It has a definitive meaning. Paying attention to ourselves means not only loving ourselves; it means giving ourselves time to grow, time to grow in every way, especially spiritually. Sometime ago, in a sermon, I talked about "letting our souls catch up with our bodies." We need to take time for that. Time to read: to read the scripture, to read devotional literature that speaks to our inner life. Time to meditate and pray. Time to worship. Occasional times for a couple of days in retreat.

We need to pay attention to ourselves by giving ourselves time.

Reflecting and Recording

Take a look at a typical week in your life. How much time do you give to yourself?

Before you started this workbook journey, what was your style of daily reading, reflection, and prayer?

Apart from eight hours working and eight hours sleeping, how do you spend the other eight hours? Are you happy with that? How much discretionary time—time you can use however you wish—do you have?

There are ways to "redeem" small blocks of time that may otherwise go for naught. One of the best ways is what I call "breathing the Presence." It requires discipline—deliberately using those "interruptions" in the flow of our day—waiting for a business appointment, standing in a checkout line of a store, in your car alone—especially waiting at a traffic light—to acknowledge God's presence, love, and care.

One of the best ways to do this is to call to mind an affirmation of scripture. This means we should memorize some of these. Isaiah 40:31 is an example. If you haven't memorized it, copy it and carry it with you, reading it at interruptions of your day until you have it memorized.

> But those who wait for the Lord shall renew their strength,
> they shall mount up with wings like eagles,
> they shall run and not be weary,
> they shall walk and not faint.
>
> —Isaiah 40:31

During the Day
Use your interruptions for "breathing the Presence."

Day Two

LET GO AND HAVE FUN

OUR THEME THIS WEEK IS "PAY ATTENTION TO YOURSELF." Yesterday, we considered the necessity of loving ourselves and giving ourselves time. Jesus said, "Love your neighbor as yourself," and the prophet Isaiah called us to "wait on the Lord." You copied this word yesterday:

But those who wait for the Lord shall renew their strength,
they shall mount up with wings like eagles,
they shall run and not be weary,
they shall walk and not faint.

—Isaiah 40:31

There is a word in Psalm 34 that also speaks to us about paying attention to ourselves: "O taste and see that the Lord is good; happy are those who take refuge in him!" (Psalm 34:8)

Taste. That's a visceral word. *Happy* suggests lightness and fun. I don't believe the psalmist would have difficulty with my contention: Paying attention to ourselves means being willing *to let go and have fun.* I believe the high level of stress in society is connected with our inability to have fun.

Now that doesn't mean we don't have leisure time or that we don't seek pleasure. We do. In fact, in his book *Is Anybody Happy?*, Norman Lobsenz says that millions of Americans are pleasure neurotics. "They think they want more leisure," he says, "but when confronted with it, they suffer from a deep psychological fear of relaxation." Drinking and smoking compulsively are just two of the ways, adds Lobsenz, that show that people don't know how to enjoy their leisure time.

Many people must first convince themselves that a form of leisure is *necessary* before they can let themselves engage in it. They will read an article if it will help them in some way. They may play tennis or golf because it is necessary for health reasons.

We often feel guilty for actually using this leisure time once we get it. Dr. Joyce Brothers wrote an article in *Parade Magazine* which she titled with the question "Do You Have Enough Fun?" One of the things she suggests as essential for relaxing fun is to get lost in the moment. "When we're truly having fun, we briefly drop out of time, focus on the moment and lose ourselves in it. We abandon ourselves to the possibility of delight at what is around us right now. We look past the serious problems, knowing they'll still be there when we come back, and take time to enjoy the positive side of life.

"Unlike the quick fix that alcohol, pills, drugs or any other addictive escape may offer, play for the sake of play doesn't leave us with withdrawal symptoms that make us anxious and desperate. Instead, it leaves us refreshed and relaxed, with a new perspective and a sharper focus" (Brothers, February 2, 1992, p. 4).

Two, Dr. Brothers says, if you don't enjoy it, don't do it. What's fun for one may be no fun at all for someone else.

She advises married couples: "Play together and stay together." She cites psychiatrist R. William Betcher, of Newton, Massachusetts, as saying that couples who frequently play together just for the fun of it are far more likely to stay together than those who don't. They take time just to be alone with one another.

We need to pay attention to ourselves by taking time to have fun.

Reflecting and Recording
Recall and record a description of your last (at least one hour) experience of "just having fun."

How long ago was the experience? Did you have difficulty calling an experience to mind? Did you resist the opportunity before it came? Did you feel guilty before or after? What do your responses to these questions tell you about your attitude about "letting go and having fun?"

♥

Ponder for a few minutes the suggestion, "if you don't enjoy it, don't do it." Have you been doing things that were *supposed to be fun,* but are not fun to you?

Spend time in prayer, making a commitment to "let go and have fun."

During the Day

Use your interruptions for "breathing the Presence." Read or quote Isaiah's word that you copied yesterday.

Day Three

THERE IS PLENTY OF WHAT YOU NEED

The point is this: the one who sows sparingly will also reap sparingly, and the one who sows bountifully will also reap bountifully. Each of you must give as you have made up your mind, not reluctantly or under compulsion, for God loves a cheerful giver. And God is able to provide you with every blessing in abundance, so that by always having enough of everything, you may share abundantly in every good work.

—2 Corinthians 9:6-8

THE WRITER ANNIE DILLARD, author of *Pilgrim at Tinker Creek,* wrote this concerning the bounty we are given:

I feel as though I stand at the foot of an infinitely high staircase, down which some exuberant spirit is flinging tennis ball after tennis ball, eternally, and the one thing I want in the world is a tennis ball. (Dillard, pp. 100-101)

We cheat ourselves by hoarding, by being fearful that there is not enough to go around: money, food, love, time, security. We need to hear Paul's word: "And God is able to provide you with every blessing in abundance, so that by always having enough of everything, you may share abundantly in every good work" (2 Cor. 9:8).

It seems to be a contradiction: *to get enough of what we need, we have to give what we need away.* Leo Buscaglia, whose story we shared on Day One, tells another story that makes my point here.

I ate recently in a real greasy spoon in Arizona. It was one of those places that you walk in and the odor is enough. Even the rats have deserted. But the food was really good. I had ordered pork chops, and somebody said, "You're crazy. You're gonna die! Nobody eats pork chops in a place like this."

I said, "But they smell so good!" And someone down at the end was having them, and he had an enormous dish! These pork chops were huge! And so I ordered the pork chops, and they were magnificent. After it was over, I said to the waitress, "You know, I'd really like to meet the chef." And she said, "Was there something wrong?"

I said, "No, I want to tell this guy how beautiful it was."

She said, "Oh, my God, no one's ever done that." And we walked back, and he was back there sweating. He was a big man.

And he said, "Whatsa matter?"

I said, "Nothing. Those pork chops were just fantastic and those potatoes! They were really wonderful. I've eaten at some of the best restaurants in the world, and they were as good."

He looked at me like, "God, this man's out of his mind." And then do you know what he said, (because it was so awkward for him to receive a compliment)—he said, "Would you like another?" Isn't that beautiful? That's love. That's all it means. It means sharing joy with people. When you see something beautiful, it means going over and telling them. When you see someone lovely, say to them, "You're lovely." And then back away! Because it's going to scare the hell out of them. (Buscaglia, pp. 251, 252)

If we are in recovery, if we are going to grow as Christians, we must pay attention to ourselves by realizing that *to get enough of what we need, we have to give what we need away.*

Reflecting and Recording

Below is a list of some of the things we need. By each one of them, make notes about your need for this particular gift: how and why you need it and whom you need it from.

Appreciation

Approval

Attention—to be listened to

Respect

Love

Look at the same list again, and make some notes about how and to whom you might give them.

Appreciation

Approval

Attention—to listen to

Respect

Love

During the Day

Put into action what you have just recorded. Select at least one person to give one of these gifts, and enjoy the response that will come.

Day Four

LIVE EXTRAVAGANTLY IN WAYS THAT MATTER

Six days before the Passover Jesus came to Bethany, the home of Lazarus, whom he had raised from the dead. There they gave a dinner for him. Martha served, and Lazarus was one of those at the table with him. Mary took a pound of costly perfume made of pure nard, anointed Jesus' feet, and wiped them with her hair. The house was filled with the fragrance of the perfume. But Judas Iscariot, one of his disciples (the one who was about to betray him), said "Why was this perfume not sold for three hundred denarii and the money given to the poor?" (He said this not because he cared about the poor, but because he was a thief; he kept the common purse and used to steal what was put into it.) Jesus said, "Leave her alone. She bought it so that she might keep it for the day of my burial. You always have the poor with you, but you do not always have me."

—John 12:1-8

THIS IS A PICTURE OF LOVE'S EXTRAVAGANCE. It's a call to us who are recovering and/or "under construction" as Christians. We need to live extravagantly in ways that matter.

We introduced this notion yesterday with the claim: *to get enough of what we need, we have to give what we need away.* This is an extravagant stance that refuses to hoard and protect ourselves.

Let's focus the principle in this way: *Give the time you think you don't have.* That's a very specific way to live extravagantly in a way that matters.

In *The Beloved Captain,* by Donald Hankey there's a passage that describes how the beloved captain cared for his men after a route march. "We all knew instinctively that he was our superior—a man of finer fibre than ourselves, a 'toff' in his own right. I suppose that was why he could be so humble without loss of dignity. For he was humble too, if that is the right word, and I think it is. No trouble of ours was too small for him to attend to. When we started route marches, for instance, and our feet were blistered and sore, as they often were at first, you would have thought that they were his own feet from the trouble he took. Of course after the march there was always an inspection of feet. That is the routine. But with him it was no mere routine. He came into our room, and, if any one had a sore foot, he would kneel down on the floor and look at it as carefully as if he had been a doctor. Then he would prescribe, and the remedies were ready at hand, being borne by a sergeant. If a blister had to be lanced, he would very likely lance it himself there and then, so as to make sure it was done with a clean needle and that no dirt was allowed to get in. There was no affectation about this, no striving after effect. It was simply that he felt that our feet were pretty important, and that he knew that we were pretty careless. So he thought it best at the start to see to the matter himself. Nevertheless, there was in our eyes something almost religious about this care for our feet. It seemed to have a touch of Christ about it, and we loved and honoured him the more." (Barclay, pp. 162, 163)

Nothing means more to persons than the attention you give them—and when the attention involves time you think you don't have, people will experience love—a love which can be the love of Christ. But, also, your life will take on a Christlike quality.

Reflecting and Recording

Recall an experience of someone giving you time they did not have. Who was that person? What did they do for a living? What did they do for you? How did it make you feel about yourself? about them?

Write enough about the story to get it fully in mind.

Spend a few minutes reflecting on your own willingness to give time you do not have.

Gratitude and praise are expressions of extravagant living. Have you ever thanked the person for the experience you just recalled? If not, and that person is still living, write or call him or her today.

During the Day

Continue the work you began yesterday of *giving what you need in order to get what you need.*

Day Five

SAY NO TO YOUR FATAL ATTRACTIONS

A MAN AT A PARTY WALKED OVER TO A WOMAN and said, "You are wearing one of the most beautiful diamond rings I have ever seen." She responded, "It's the Chapman diamond, and a curse comes with it."

Backing off a bit, the man asked, "What is the curse?"

The woman frowned and replied, "Mr. Chapman, who gave it to me."

That's a telling commentary on life. Sometimes the price we pay for things is too great. And it's not always as obvious and dramatic as the curse of the Chapman diamond.

We can sell our integrity for money. We can sell our sense of self-worth by doing the expected things to fit in. We can sell our capacity to dream by settling for security. We can sell our character by compromising our values.

The death and resurrection of Jesus Christ is at the heart of the Christian faith. Death and resurrection is also the pattern for Christian living. There are things we must die to in order to come alive and grow spiritually and emotionally. This was the dynamic witness of Paul, the Apostle.

For through the law I died to the law, so that I might live to God. I have been crucified with Christ; and it is no longer I who live, but it is Christ who lives in me. And the life I now live in the flesh I live by faith in the Son of God, who loved me and gave himself for me.

—Galatians 2:19-20

In his letter to the Colossians, he used this same image.

So if you have been raised with Christ, seek the things that are above, where Christ is, seated at the right hand of God. Set your minds on things that are above, not on things that are on earth, for you have died, and your life is hidden with Christ in God. When Christ who is your life is revealed, then you also will be revealed with him in glory.

Put to death, therefore, whatever in you is earthly: fornication, impurity, passion, evil desire, and greed (which is idolatry). On account of these the wrath of God is coming on those who are disobedient. These are the ways you also once followed, when you were living that life. But now you must get rid of all such things—anger, wrath, malice, slander, and abusive language from your mouth.

—Colossians 3:1-8

Our life as Christians, then, is a life of dying to old crippling habits, destructive patterns of relating, and self-defeating behavior and coming alive to the *new life* that is being birthed through the power of Christ within. Discipline is required. However, it is a discipline that brings life and joy.

So if you are going to pay attention to yourself, you must *say no to your fatal attractions*. For some, money is a fatal attraction. They seem never to be able to deal with it.

For others, it is success and ambition. Their identity is tied to performance, what they achieve.

For others, it is sex. They think it is impossible to live without a sexual relationship, and many of their problems come from this undisciplined drive being satisfied outside the covenant of marriage.

Many addictive persons live with the phenomena of being instinctively and powerfully attracted to people who are not in their best interest. Melody Beattie shares the confession of persons for whom relationships always seem destructive, if not fatal.

> "I can walk into a room of 500 men, 499 of whom are successful and healthy, spot the one unemployed felon in the bunch, and find him catching my eye," says Christy.
>
> "When I met my ex-husband, a raving sex addict and alcoholic, my first thought was, *This guy looks like trouble.* My second thought was, *Let me at him!*" says Jan.
>
> "There's something compelling about a woman who looks like she might 'do me wrong,' " says Don. "I've been recovering for years, and that's the kind of woman I'm still drawn to." (Beattie, p. 151)

Money, success, ambition, sex, relationships, and we could go on and on. There are attractions that can be destructive. We need to recognize these and say *no* to them in order to say *yes* to that which contributes to our health and wholeness.

The slogan "Just Say No!" may be a bit superficial, if we think it is easy. But there is truth in that slogan. A bank president was having an affair with a female employee, and this created all sorts of problems for the bank. The board of directors hired a psychologist to consult with them and to offer advice about the situation. After about two hours of discussion, they asked the psychologist to give his opinion. He said, "Tell him to stop it."

The board members were stunned with the simple answer. They had paid this fellow good money, and this was all the advice he was offering?

They called the president into the meeting and simply told him to stop the affair.

An interesting thing happened. The president was more than willing to abide by the decision.

Deep down we know that whenever we are doing wrong, or intend to do something wrong, the solution is to stop it.

Reflecting and Recording

Some of us struggle with *fatal* attractions. Many of us struggle with *destructive* attractions. Perhaps most of us are at least aware of *unhealthy* attractions.

Make a list of your fatal, destructive, or unhealthy attractions.

1.

2.

3.

4.

Go back to the list above and make some notes on how these are plaguing you, doing damage, or preventing spiritual, emotional, or relational growth.

Overcoming our fatal attractions is more often a process than a one-time victory. Though it does happen, rare is the experience of a person being instantaneously delivered from dominant drives and passions that have been exercised and fed for so long. However, miraculous change is not only possible, it is the norm of disciplined Christian living. We need to be honest about our fatal attractions, try to avoid persons, places, and circumstances that feed these attractions, guard against temptations, confess to Christ and to our supportive community, and depend on Christ's power to say no until the "attraction" no longer attracts.

Write a brief prayer of confession and commitment in relation to your attraction.

During the Day

Jesus said, "The gate is wide and the road is easy that leads to destruction" (Matt. 7:13). Take this thought with you today.

Day Six

GOD'S LOVE IS NOT FICKLE

What then are we to say about these things? If God is for us, who is against us? He who did not withhold his own Son, but gave him up for all of us, will he not with him also give us everything else? Who will bring any charge against God's elect? It is God who justifies. Who is to condemn? It is Christ Jesus, who died, yes, who was raised, who is at the right hand of God, who indeed intercedes for us. Who will separate us from the love of Christ? Will hardship, or distress, or persecution, or famine, or nakedness, or peril, or sword? As it is written,
"For your sake we are being killed all day long;
 we are accounted as sheep to be slaughtered."
No, in all these things we are more than conquerors, through him who loved us. For I am convinced that neither death, nor life, nor angels, nor rulers, nor things present, nor things to come, nor powers, nor height, nor depth, nor anything else in all creation, will be able to separate us from the love of God in Christ Jesus our Lord.

—Romans 8:31-39

Eileen Freeman tells about leading a retreat for Catholic senior high school girls. They were having a discussion on the pains and joys of growing up. The girls said their greatest worry was the fear of getting married because they were afraid their husbands would stop loving them someday.

Freeman said, "That is one of the saddest things I have ever heard. . . . it is bad enough to grow up in a society like ours where so many of the ills are mostly impersonal, but if someone stops loving you, that's personal. Not to be loved by a human being would be the worst thing."

My preacher friend, Rodney Wilmoth, who told this story said:

We know that human love can be quite fickle. But Paul's point is that his certainty is in the knowledge that nothing will ever be able to separate us from the love of God. God's love is not fickle. Nothing will ever be able to separate us from that love.

And what gives Paul this confidence and this certainty? His own personal experience. Paul's entire life as a missionary was sustained by the assurance of the crucifixion and resurrection of Jesus Christ.

Jesus Christ was for Paul acquired immunity. It did not mean that Paul breezed through life unscathed. Paul endured many things. He certainly was not inoculated from life's difficult moments, but he was immune to defeat for he had the confidence and certainty that Christ would sustain him. That is acquired immunity in its finest sense! (Wilmoth, August 5, 1990)

We can be certain that God's love is not fickle. Nothing will provide more sustaining power in our lives than this confidence.

Do you remember Father Lawrence Jenco? He spent many long months as a prisoner of Lebanese terrorists a few years ago.

Jenco tells of how he was bound and trussed like a turkey and shoved into a rack beneath a flatbed truck where the spare tire is usually stored. Apparently his captors were taking him to a new place of hiding. Father Jenco felt certain that they were taking him out to kill him.

On that awful ride, he remembers saying these words to himself: "I am a being of worth and dignity. I belong to God. I am redeemed."

He prayed words like these from the Psalms: "Yea, though I walk through the valley of the shadow of death, I shall fear no evil. FOR THOU ART WITH ME." He remembers reflecting upon the words of Jesus, "Lo, I am with you always to the close of the age."

Father Jenco knew what we must know and always remember: God's love is not fickle.

Reflecting and Recording

Recall and describe an experience when you were sustained by confidence in the love, presence, and power of God. Write enough details to relive the experience.

Is there anything in your life now with which you could cope better if you relied more on God's love, presence, and power?

During the Day

If you know someone who would profit from hearing your experience of God's love, presence, and power, share it with him or her by letter or telephone today.

Day Seven

CLAIM WHO YOU ARE AS A CHILD OF THE KING

For if one man's offence meant that men should be slaves to death all their lives, it is a far greater thing that through another man, Jesus Christ, men by their acceptance of his more than sufficient grace and righteousness, should live their lives victoriously.

We see then that as one act of sin exposed the whole race of men to God's judgment and condemnation, so one act of perfect righteousness presents all men freely acquitted in the sight of God. One man's disobedience placed all men under the threat of condemnation, but one man's obedience has the power to present all men righteous before God.

Now we find that the Law keeps slipping into the picture to point out the vast extent of sin. Yet, though sin is shown to be wide and deep, thank God his grace is wider and deeper still! The whole outlook changes—sin used to be the master of men and in the end handed them over to death; now grace is the ruling factor, with its purpose making men right with God and its end the bringing of them to eternal life through Jesus Christ our Lord.

—Romans 5:16-20, PHILLIPS

HAVE YOU EVER CONSIDERED THE POSSIBILITY of living your life as a king?

Oswald Sanders, in *Spiritual Maturity* (Chicago: Moody, p. 125), makes this comment on the above scripture passage: "What a fascinating picture of Christian living this vivid picture portrays: nobility, charm, authority, wealth, freedom. Our God invites us to believe that these spiritual qualities are prerogatives and prerogatives may and should be enjoyed by every child of the King of Kings. If you do not manifest and enjoy them, it is not because they are beyond our reach, but only because we're living below our privileges."

What a fact to celebrate! What a promise to claim! As Christians we are children of the King.

Somewhere I read about a technique used to catch monkeys in the jungle. A hole is drilled in a coconut, and food is placed inside. The hole must be large enough for the monkey to get his hand in, but small enough that he cannot get it out once he grabs the food. The coconut is chained to the coconut tree. Once the monkey grasps the food, he is stuck. Refusing to let the food go, he is in bondage to the coconut. The hunters simply have to come and collect the monkeys who, by their own choice, are bound.

It's a parable for us as Christians under construction and/or in recovery; we must *let go* of a lot of things. As we considered on Day Five, the rhythm of Christian recovery and growth is death and resurrection. I was shocked recently when the thought came to me that Jesus never went to a funeral. He did show up at places where people had died—but he showed up there to give them life. He performed his first miracle at a wedding feast.

Jesus was not calloused about grief and sorrow. He went when he heard of his friend Lazarus's death. But his focus was not on grief and loss and death, but on life. So we must *let go* of those things in our past that continue to weigh us down; let go of those forces that have our lives in hock; those destructive habits and attitudes that keep robbing us of new possibility, hope, and life. We are children of the King, and all the grace of God is available to us.

Ruth Graham, the wife of evangelist Billy Graham, decided what she wanted to have written on her tombstone when she dies. It's not what you would expect at all, a most unusual statement indeed. She saw it one day on a road sign when she and Billy were driving in their car. They had gone through several miles of road construction where they had to slow down and drive in a single lane and take a detour here and there. But finally they came to the end of the construction, and there

Ruth saw the sign that caught her attention. "That's what I want on my tombstone," she said to Billy, pointing at the sign. And at first he didn't get it, but then it began to dawn on him and he smiled. You know what the sign said, the words that Ruth wants on her tombstone? It is this— "End of construction. Thanks for your patience."

Isn't that wonderful? "End of construction. Thanks for your patience." You see, God is the one who is creating all of us all of the time. God is not simply the one who created us long ago and threw us out into the world and left us to fend for ourselves. No, God is still in the process of creating us, each one of us. We must keep on trusting him, for we are Christians under construction and in recovery.

Reflecting and Recording

Since this the last day in this workbook adventure, spend some time looking back over your experience of the past seven weeks. Make some notes about new discoveries you have made about yourself, new insight, new possibilities for the future, breaks and freedom from the past, new learnings, new direction for relationships—things that you need to remember as you live as a Christian under construction and/or in recovery.

During the Day—and all days to come

Remember you are more than you think you are, and there is something you can be, but will never be apart from Jesus Christ.

GROUP MEETING FOR WEEK SEVEN

NOTE: The leader for this week should bring a chalkboard or newsprint to the meeting. Read number 6 of "Sharing Together."

Introduction

This is the last meeting designed for this group. You may have already talked about the possibility of continuing to meet. You should conclude those plans. Some groups find it meaningful to select two or three weeks of the workbook and go through those weeks again as an extension of time together. Others continue for an additional set time, using other resources.

Whatever you choose to do, it is usually helpful to determine the actual timeline so that persons can make a clear commitment.

Another possibility that has been very effective in our congregation in Memphis is for one or two persons to decide they will recruit and lead a group of new persons through the workbook. Many people are looking for a small group growth experience, and this is a way to respond to that need.

Sharing Together

1. Begin your sharing by inviting two or three people to take a minute or two sharing their most enjoyable recent experience of "just having fun."

Following the sharing of these personal experiences, take an additional five to ten minutes for the group to discuss the importance of "having fun."

2. Day One of this week introduced the notion that we must pay attention to ourselves. We considered this same idea from another perspective on Day Four of Week Two: "Being good is bad for you when you compulsively care for others, but ignore caring for yourself."

For some this seems selfish, and even a violation of Jesus' call to "give ourselves away." Spend eight to ten minutes discussing this idea. Especially encourage persons who have difficulty "taking care of themselves" to share their experience. Be sure to *force* the questions: Do we really love ourselves? Do we give ourselves time?

3. The primary lesson for Day Four was "we cheat ourselves by hoarding." If anyone has difficulty with that notion or other ideas expressed in the context of Day Three, invite them to raise questions with the group.

4. Turn to page 151 where you reflected and recorded about things you need. Move through each of the gifts listed, (approval, attention . . .), talking briefly about our need for these gifts. Then focus conversation on the second part of the exercises: "how and to whom you might give these gifts."

4A. Are there other things you need that you also need to give away?

5. Invite a person or two to share their experience of someone giving them time they did not have. (Day Four)

6. Ask the group to look at the "fatal attractions" they recorded on Day 5. Leader, write these on a chalkboard or newsprint as they are called out by persons. When the list is completed, go back and take a count of how many named a particular "fatal attraction."

A. Spend a few minutes talking about those "attractions" that were listed the most and the least number of times.

B. Talk about how some of these attractions listed may be "unhealthy," though not "destructive."

C. Invite two or three persons who are willing to share their struggle with some "fatal" attractions, especially share the help they are receiving for dealing with it.

D. Invite someone to share the prayer of confession and commitment in relation to their "attraction." Do not feel badly if no one shares. Many times we are not ready to share our prayers at the point of our deepest personal struggle, even with our closest friends. That's okay, but we also need to remember that being open and vulnerable is also a ministry to others as well as healing to us.

7. Invite one person to share an experience when he or she was sustained by the confidence of God's presence, love, and power.

8. Use the balance of your discussion time (save time for prayer) for persons to share the meaning of this seven-week journey, questions they have, insights they have received, changes that have occurred, commitments they have made.

Praying Together

1. Begin your time of prayer by asking as many persons as will to express gratitude to God in a two- or three-sentence prayer for something significant that has happened to him or her as a result of these seven weeks.

2. Give each person the opportunity to share whatever decision or commitment he or she has made, or will make, to an ongoing life of

construction and recovery. Be specific. Follow each person's verbalizing of these decisions and commitments by having some other person in the group offer a brief prayer of thanksgiving and support for this person.

3. A benediction is a blessing or greeting shared with another or by a group in parting. The "passing of the peace" is such a benediction. You take a person's hand, look into his or her eyes and say, "The peace of the Lord be with you," and the person responds, "And the Lord's peace be yours." Then that person, taking the hands of the person next to him or her says, "The peace of the Lord be yours." Standing in a circle, let the leader "pass the peace," and let it go around the circle.

4. Having completed the passing of the peace, speak to one another in a more spontaneous way. Move about to different persons in the group, saying whatever you feel is appropriate for your parting blessing to each person. Or, you may simply embrace the person and say nothing. In your own unique way, "bless" each person who has shared this journey with you.

Notes

Sources quoted in this workbook are identified by author and page number. Bibliographic information for each source is listed below.

Barclay, William. *The Gospel of John, vol. 2.* Rev. ed. Philadelphia: The Westminster Press, 1975.

Bauknight, Brian K. "Barn Raising?" (unpublished sermon) February 26, 1989.

Beattie, Melody. *Beyond Codependency and Getting Better All the Time.* San Francisco: Harper & Row, 1989.

Buscaglia, Leo. *Living, Loving and Learning.* New York: Ballentine Books, 1983.

Carter, Les. *Putting the Past Behind.* Chicago: Moody Press, 1989.

Chambers, Oswald. *My Utmost for His Highest.* London: Simpkin Marshall, Ltd., 1937.

Dillard, Annie. *Pilgrim at Tinker Creek.* New York: Harper's Magazine Press, 1974.

Dunnam, Maxie. *Be Your Whole Self.* Old Tappan, NJ: Fleming H. Revell Company, 1970.

Hemfelt, Robert, Minirth, Frank, and Meier, Paul. *Love Is a Choice.* Nashville: Thomas Nelson, Inc. 1989.

Hinson, William H. *Solid Living in a Shattered World.* Nashville: Abingdon Press, 1985.

Menninger, Karl. *Whatever Became of Sin?* New York: Hawthorn Books, 1973.

Muggeridge, Malcolm. *Jesus, the Man Who Lives.* New York: Harper & Row, 1975.

Olmstead, Bob. "When Being Good Is Bad for You" (unpublished sermon) June 24, 1990.

Ortlund, Anne. *Disciplines of the Heart.* Waco, TX: Word Books, 1987.

Schmidt, Kenneth A. *Finding Your Way Home.* Ventura, CA: Regal Books, 1990.

Seamands, David A. *Healing for Damaged Emotions.* Wheaton, IL: Victor Books, 1991.

Seamands, David A. *Healing Grace.* Wheaton, IL: Victor Books, 1988.

Shelby, Donald. "On Being Assertive" (unpublished sermon) August 16, 1981.

Wilmoth, Rodney E. "Acquired Immunity" (unpublished sermon) August 5, 1990.